OIL IN CHINA

From Self-Reliance to Internationalization

Series on Contemporary China (ISSN: 1793-0847)

Series Editors: Joseph Fewsmith *(Boston University)*
Zheng Yongnian *(East Asian Institute, National University of Singapore)*

*Published**

Vol. 6 Water and Development in China: The Political Economy of Shanghai Water Policy
by Seungho Lee

Vol. 7 De Facto Federalism in China: Reforms and Dynamics of Central-Local Relations
by Zheng Yongnian

Vol. 8 China's Elite Politics: Political Transition and Power Balancing
by Bo Zhiyue

Vol. 9 Economic Reform and Cross-Strait Relations: Taiwan and China in the WTO
edited by Julian Chang & Steven M Goldstein

Vol. 10 Discontented Miracle: Growth, Conflict, and Institutional Adaptations in China
edited by Dali L Yang

Vol. 11 China's Surging Economy: Adjusting for More Balanced Development
edited by John Wong & Wei Liu

Vol. 12 Tobacco Control Policy Analysis in China: Economics and Health
edited by Teh-Wei Hu

Vol. 13 China's Science and Technology Sector and the Forces of Globalisation
edited by Elspeth Thomson & Jon Sigurdson

Vol. 14 Migration and Social Protection in China
edited by Ingrid Nielsen & Russell Smyth

Vol. 15 China's Reforms at 30: Challenges and Prospects
edited by Dali L Yang & Litao Zhao

Vol. 16 Political Booms: Local Money and Power in Taiwan, East China, Thailand and the Philippines
by Lynn T White

Vol. 17 Politics of China's Environmental Protection: Problems and Progress
by Chen Gang

Vol. 18 Oil in China: From Self-Reliance to Internationalization
by Lim Tai Wei

*To view the complete list of the published volumes in the series, please visit:
http://www.worldscibooks.com/series/scc_series.shtml

Series on Contemporary China – Vol. 18

OIL IN CHINA

From Self-Reliance to Internationalization

Lim Tai Wei

East Asian Institute,

National University of Singapore, Singapore

NEW JERSEY • LONDON • SINGAPORE • BEIJING • SHANGHAI • HONG KONG • TAIPEI • CHENNAI

Published by

World Scientific Publishing Co. Pte. Ltd.
5 Toh Tuck Link, Singapore 596224
USA office: 27 Warren Street, Suite 401-402, Hackensack, NJ 07601
UK office: 57 Shelton Street, Covent Garden, London WC2H 9HE

British Library Cataloguing-in-Publication Data
A catalogue record for this book is available from the British Library.

Series on Contemporary China — Vol. 18
OIL IN CHINA
From Self-Reliance to Internationalization

ISBN-13 978-981-4273-76-3
ISBN-10 981-4273-76-7

Typeset by Stallion Press
E-mail: enquiries@stallionpress.com

Printed in Singapore by B & Jo Enterprise Pte Ltd

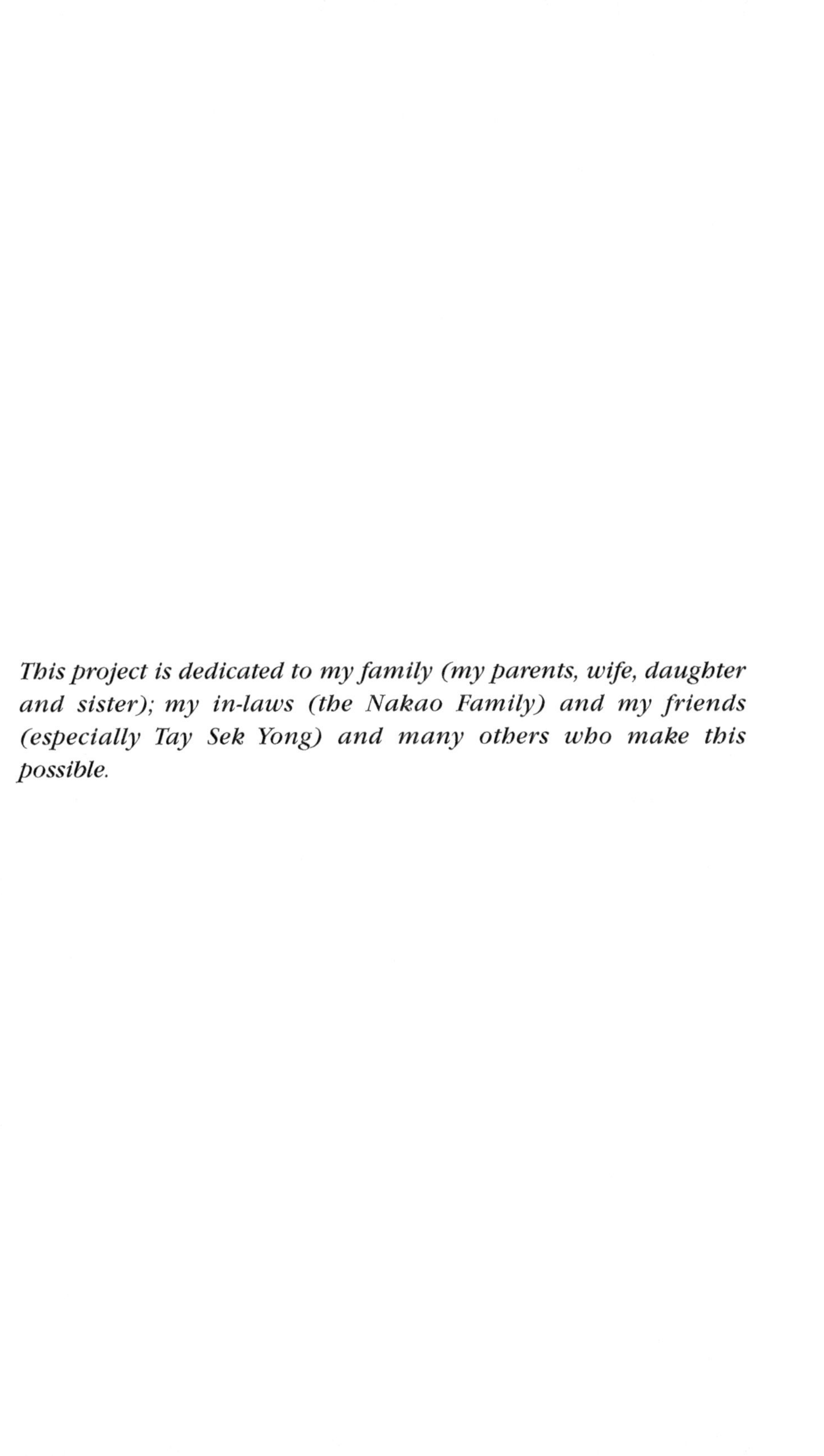

This project is dedicated to my family (my parents, wife, daughter and sister); my in-laws (the Nakao Family) and my friends (especially Tay Sek Yong) and many others who make this possible.

Preface

This monograph seeks to analyze key historical developmental concepts and events in the Chinese oil industry, namely the concepts of self-reliance, Sino-Japanese oil trade and the transition from self-reliance to internationalization, from the establishment of the Daqing oilfield to its early days of internationalization. These themes will be examined in the subsequent chapters and are embedded within the empirical case study of Daqing, PRC's premiere oilfield for most of the postwar period and a symbol of industrialization and self-reliance in the PRC. In the process of examining the selected themes, Japan's role in stimulating the development of the Chinese oil industry will also be highlighted as the Japanese state and its business sectors emerged as a supplier of technology and equipment to the Chinese oil industry and its first major oil customer in the early internationalization phase of the PRC oil industry. The political and conceptual metamorphosis of self-reliance to internationalization will also be examined in this project.

About the Author

LIM Tai Wei has a LLB (Hons) from the University of London, a BA (Merit) in double majors Political Science and Japanese Studies with a minor in History and a BA (First Class Honors) in Japanese Studies from the National University of Singapore (NUS). He has an MA (Japanese Studies) from NUS and MA (History) and PhD from Cornell University.

Contents

Preface vii

About the Author ix

Chapter 1. Introduction 1

Chapter 2. The Founding of Daqing 9

Chapter 3. Daqing-ism 33

Chapter 4. The Doctrine of Self-Reliance 57

Chapter 5. The Cultural Revolution Interregnum 79

Chapter 6. Looking Beyond Self-Reliance 107

Chapter 7. Reliance on Japan 121

Chapter 8. Conclusion 151

Bibliography 161

Index 169

Chapter

1

Introduction

This project seeks to analyze key historical developmental concepts and events in the Chinese oil industry: namely the concepts of self-reliance, Sino-Japanese oil trade and the transition from self-reliance to internationalization; from the establishment of the Daqing oilfield to its early days of internationalization. These themes will be examined in the subsequent chapters and are embedded within the empirical case study of Daqing, the People's Republic of China (PRCs) premiere oilfield for most of the postwar period and a symbol of industrialization and self-reliance in the country. In the process of examining the selected themes, Japan's role in stimulating the development of the Chinese oil industry will also be highlighted as the Japanese state and its business sectors emerged as a supplier of technology and equipment to the Chinese oil industry and its first major oil customer in the early internationalization phase of the industry. The political and conceptual metamorphosis of self-reliance to internationalization will also be examined in this project.

At the founding of the PRC, China's oilfields were producing an annual output of 120 000 tons and, even in 1952, oil production constituted only 1.3 percent of China's total energy production.[1] But, in 1960 with the discovery of Daqing, China saw hope for oil self-reliance for the first time. Crude oil production attained six million tons in less than four years.[2] Thirteen years after the discovery of Daqing in 1960, China's crude oil output reached 100 million[3] by the time China was ready to export its oil resource to the outside world with the US recognition of China in 1972 and the open-door policy in 1978. Daqing was one of the main propelling forces pushing China's ranking in terms of global oil production from 12th in 1965 to 8th in 1978, 6th in the 1980s and 5th in 1990 ranked after the familiar names in global oil production like Saudi Arabia, US, Russia and Iran.[4]

Daqing was also the PRC's first indigenously-designed oil complex.[5] The spatial construction of Daqing was deliberately conceived and purposeful. The oilfield facility is spacious,[6] much like Manchuria with its wide open space for settlers. It was an empty flat land waiting to be subjugated and settled. The whole facility was a curious mix of urbanization and rural environmentalism. Daqing had a feel of utopian camaraderie and enjoyed high morale. Daqing's successes became a source of pride for China's oil bureaucracy and also generated a great sense of confidence amongst its staff. With great progress made in Daqing, Yu Qiuli (Daqing's first manager) won acclaim from Mao Zedong who called on the whole nation to emulate the organizational principles of Daqing. Mao was so impressed by Yu and his work at Daqing that, when he became disenchanted with

---

[1] Wong, J. and Wong, C. K. (1998). *China's New Oil Development Strategy Taking Shape*, p. 12. Singapore: World Scientific.

[2] Ibid.

[3] Ibid., p. 13.

[4] Thomson, E. (2001). *China's Growing Dependence on Oil Imports EAI Background Brief No. 87*, p. 2. Singapore: East Asian Institute.

[5] Zhongguo Lianyou Gongye (China Oil-Refining Industry) Editorial Team (1989). *Zhongguo Lianyou Gongye (China Oil-Refining Industry)*, p. 408. China: Shiyou Gongye Chubanshe.

[6] Bartke, W. (1977). *Oil in the People's Republic of China*, p. 75. Montreal: McGill-Queens University Press.

economic progress in the 3rd five-year plan for the oil industry, he turned to Yu Qiuli to head a new planning group and named Kang Shien a member of this group.[7]

The technocratic (Yu)-ideological (Mao) alliance disseminated images of Daqing development to all walks of life. Both groups were instrumental in supplying the enormous resources necessary for Daqing's development. The technocracy and their expert knowledge were needed to resolve the contradiction and gap between ideological modernization and material progress. Oil and the modern processes it powered was necessary to support the Communist Revolution with the eradication of backwardness and self-strengthening as part of its aims.

To a large extent, when oil first gushed out, Daqing's victorious construction also took hold of the realm of imagination. It was as much about imaginative projection, and symbol-making as the material process itself. Ideological ideas about what Daqing potentially represented shaped the appropriation of its use in the public imaginative realm. Imaginative projections continuously interacted with public perceptions. The mere discovery incited exuberance that became infectious and generated high hopes for the project. As Daqing performed quantitatively, it drew in an increasingly inclusive participation of Chinese society.

The Daqing movement went on to mobilize the energies of workers, agriculturalists, technocrats, planners in other sectors of the Chinese economy and society. From top down to bottom up, agents of Daqing sought to involve all sections of Chinese society in the project. A variety of organizations and people played a role in the ongoing process of mobilization for oil self-reliance. Daqing-era oil industry literature stated that self-reliance did not just apply to vital industrial process and machineries but also included peripheral functions like haircutting and instituting mutual assistance amongst workers to help

---

[7] Lieberthal, K. and Oksenberg, M. (1986). *Bureaucratic Politics and Chinese Energy Development*, p. 67. Prepared for the Department of Commerce Contract No. 50-SATA-4-16230. Washington: Center for Chinese Studies, The University of Michigan.

each other cut their hair.[8] Even in popular folklore, the glorification of Model Worker Wang Jinxi elucidated the popular reading of the Daqing phenomenon. In a scene from the movie, *Daqing Shiyou Huizhan*, Ironman Wang was seen heroically drenched in mud in a pit during an excavation.[9] Such popular readings of Daqing provided the primary medium through which cross-sections of Chinese society would experience Daqing.

DECLARATION OF SELF-RELIANCE

Daqing's discovery made it possible for the Chinese leadership to declare that they were now "self-reliant" in their supply of oil. Zhou Enlai's famous oil self-reliance remarks were declared at the Second National People's Congress on 17 November 1963 against the backdrop of "a sunlit large five-star banner (China's national flag) embodying the most cherished essence of Oriental peoples."[10] The powerful imagery also described as a "glorious war result (*huihuang de zhanji*)" was constructed as a befitting end to the "Eastern giant's (*dongfang daguo*)" longstanding slavish dependence ("*yangrenbixi*") on foreign oil supplies.[11]

In that speech which was released to the Second National People's Congress (*Quanguo Renda Erjie Shichi Huiyi*) held between 17 November to 3 December 1963, Zhou Enlai said: "Because of the discovery and construction of the Daqing oilfield, our country's economic construction, the oil needs of defense and civilian applications which had depended on foreign imports in the past, are now basically self-reliant, whether in volume or in variety. (*Youyu Daqing youtian de faxian he jiancheng, woguo jingji*

[8] Li, C. (1977). *Yi "Lianglun" Wei Zhidao, Jiansheguodeying de Jichendui* (*Using the "Two Theories" as Guidance, to Build a Solid Grassroot Team*), p. 83. China: Renminchubanshe.

[9] Tatsu, K. (2002). *Chugoku no Sekiyuu to Tenran Gasu* (*China's Oil and Natural Gas*), p. 18. Japan: Institute of Development Economies.

[10] Chen, D.K. (1994). *Zhongguo Shiyou Dahui Zhan* (*A Chinese Great Battle for Oil*), p. 300. China: Bayi Chubanshe.

[11] Ibid., p. 304.

jianshe, guofang jianshe he renmin xuyong de shiyou, guoqu dabufen yikao jingkou, xianzai buguan shizai shuliangshang huozhezai pinzhongshang, dou yijing jiben zhigeile)".[12]

Daqing is widely acknowledged by both foreign and domestic observers intimate with the Chinese oil industry to be the main contributing factor to China's success in becoming basically self-reliant in 1962. China's oil self-reliance is usually judged by the amount of its oil imports which showed a dramatic reduction from 1962. This was not the only standard that can be used to judge China's self-reliance in oil. In fact, of greater strategic concern to China's planners, perhaps, was self-reliance in military-grade oil, particularly those used by China's aviation industry and air force. Overall, Daqing's symbolism of self-reliance was augmented by the fact that China produced 30 million tons in 1972 or 1.1 percent of the world's total output of oil and her oil production global ranking increased by 16 percent between 1971 and 1972, occupying the sixth place after Algeria (43.1 percent), Saudi Arabia (27.7 percent), Indonesia (21.3 percent), Nigeria (18.8 percent) and Canada (16.6 percent).[13]

The chronological evolution of self-reliance perhaps reached its zenith in the PRC when the cherished aim of self-reliance was vigorously projected onto all Chinese industries through the "Learn from Daqing" conferences. Daqing-ism meant "getting every enterprise to emulate Taching [Daqing] and work hard and self-reliantly".[14] Self-reliance had evolved to become a value system in Daqing. It embodied and became defined as a national culture through which a collective or communal identity can be constructed and highlighted. The doctrine was freed of its spatial limitations and was allowed to blossom extensively. The doctrine of self-reliance also

---

[12] Wen, H., Wang, Z., Zhang, J., Guan, X., Liu, M., Chen, Z., Dai, N., Nan, Y., Wu, Q., Zhang, S. and Wang, S. (2002). *Bainian Shiyou (100 Years of Petroleum),* 1878–2000, p. 156. China: Dangdai Zhongguo Chubanshe.

[13] Bartke, W. (1977). *Oil in the People's Republic of China*, p. 45. Montreal: McGill-Queens University Press.

[14] Foreign Languages Press (1977). *The National Conference on Learning from Taching in Industry Selected Documents,* p. 67. Beijing: Foreign Languages Press.

acted as an ordering and bordering ideology within the national imagination against foreign reliance.

Every successive Chinese leader has tried to claim the credit for China's oil self-reliance. Chairman Hua Guofeng, successor to Mao Zedong, declared at the National Conference on Learning from Taching (Daqing) in Industry in 1977 that, under his watch and other senior leaders, Daqing became "one of the world's few huge oilfields at high speed, thus ridding China once and for all of backwardness in the petroleum industry and ending the days when China had to depend on imported oil. Taching's (Daqing's) petroleum output has been rising steadily over the past 17 years at an average annual increase of 28 percent. The present Taching (Daqing) is equivalent to six Tachings (Daqings) in 1965, the year before the start of the Great Cultural Revolution… It has its own unique creations, many of which are up to or surpass the most advanced world standards."[15] He credited his administration for restoring Chinese oil self-reliance again after production declined during the Cultural Revolution, adding his legacy to the long-vaunted goal of Chinese oil resource nationalism.

While the multitude of terms and explanations for self-reliance point to its appropriation by different Chinese factions, it also underlines the evolutionary nature of the term and the continuity that underlies this process through what would generally be classified as sharp discontinuities in Chinese oil history. The element of self-reliance showed continuity in contextual readings of oil development in China. Self-reliance mitigates and smoothens out these sharp discontinuities into meandering contours in Chinese industrial history. The multiplicity of meanings of the term self-reliance was sometimes obscured, ignored or intentionally made amorphous so that terms could be made adaptable and acceptable under different regimes, times, regions and environments.

But care was taken throughout to ensure that exceptions applied to self-reliance. For example, in 1965, Mao enunciated the idea that it was not against self-reliance to have international assistance.

---

[15] Ibid., p. 11.

His views were printed in the Peking Review: "While adhering to the policy of self-reliance in our socialist construction, we have highly valued and welcomed international assistance... China cannot procure funds for construction by contracting enslaving foreign loans at the expense of her sovereignty and independence... We rely solely on international accumulation of funds for large-scale construction."[16] This line was seized on by reformers in the post-Maoist era who then argued that self-reliance and foreign trade were not mutually exclusive.[17] Such pragmatic thinking endured even during the era of the Gang of Four in the Cultural Revolution when it was argued that foreign technology and equipment should be imported and made to serve China (*Yangwei Zhongyong*).[18]

In the post-Mao era, the ability to accommodate foreign help into self-reliance as and when the situation necessitated it was developed much further by Deng Xiaoping who went before the Sixth Special Session of the UN General Assembly on 10 April 1974 and said: "By self-reliance we mean that a country should rely on the strength and wisdom of its own people, control its own resources, strive hard to increase food production, and develop its national economy step by step in a planned way."[19] He also argued that self-reliance did not rule out foreign help in achieving such goals. In Deng's time, these arguments were prompted by post-Cultural Revolution economic pressures which were beginning to mount on the Chinese side as well.

This was a significant paradigm shift since, at the founding of the People's Republic of China, one of the central tenets of the communist doctrine was self-reliance which included resisting the influx of foreign or capitalist finances. Even as late as 1977, the Chinese government mouthpiece, *People's Daily*, insisted that China should not permit any foreign interests (including jointly-managed companies)

[16] Lee, T. H. (1995). *Politics of Energy Policy in Post-Mao China,* p. 180. Korea: Asiatic Research Center, Korea University.

[17] Ibid., p. 188.

[18] Ibid.

[19] Ibid.

from touching Chinese raw materials.[20] However, this doctrine became increasingly difficult to uphold, particularly after the economically devastating Cultural Revolution in the 1970s.

The concept of self-reliance was molded and modified to fit changing circumstances brought about by international trade in oil with the Japanese. Neither Daqing's demonstration of superhuman efforts by workers like Ironman Wang nor makeshift equipment could hold off equipment modernization entirely without the help of foreign input and advanced technologies. Although China mastered basic oil technologies or had adapted them from foreign sources, their equipment were found wanting as China's economy opened up to the world. The re-configuration of self-reliance from being dependent on one's resources and capability and oil production for domestic uses to the institution of high-volume production for exportation and the influx of foreign technological assistance will be studied in detail in the subsequent chapters.

After the introductory chapter, the next section of the book will outline the founding of the Daqing oilfield. Chapter Three surveys how Daqing's numerical successes translated into the transformation of the oilfield into an ideology, serving as a model for heavy industrial development. This phase of Daqing development represented the peak of its model status. In Chapter Four, central to the ideology of Daqing-ism, is the concept of self-reliance in an era of PRC development where foreign technological help was extremely limited. Chapter Five analyzes the onset and impact of the Cultural Revolution. When Mao's social experimentation was finally over, Chapter Six examines how the oil industry's Petroleum Faction returned to power again with a conscious re-configuration of the self-reliance doctrine. Chapter Seven looks at the limitations of self-reliance and how it finally gave way to an oil trade with Japan, its first foreign partner in the oil industry since the Sino-Soviet split.

[20] Newby, L. (1988). *Sino-Japanese Relations*, p. 39. London: Routledge.

Chapter

2

The Founding of Daqing

DAQING

Daqing is located in a large kidney-shaped plateau between the Songhua River and Nunjiang River in Heilongjiang Province and is outlined by Fuyu (Fuyu), Dakang (Taikang) and Majiayao (Machiayao).[1] It spans an area that covers 250 km from north to south with its most oil-rich region covering a total of 50,000 square kilometers.[2] Current literature revises Daqing's size downwards to 10,000 square kilometers, 138 km north to south and 73 km east to west.[3] Before it was revealed publicly in 1964, Daqing's exact location was the subject of intense speculation. The prestigious *Oil and Gas Journal* in the US placed Daqing 500 miles southwest of its exact

---

[1] Cheng, C. (1976). *China's Petroleum Industry,* p. 57. New York: Praeger.

[2] Ling, H. C. (1975). *The Petroleum Industry of the People's Republic of China,* p. 126. Stanford: Hoover Institution Press.

[3] Zhang, S. (1988). *Yumen Youkuangshi (A History of Yumen Oil Field) 1939–1949,* p. 138. China: Xibei Daxue Chubanshe Xibei University Press.

location while *Talu Wenti Chuanti Yenchiu* in Taiwan cited Japanese sources that pinpoint Daqing to a similarly mistaken location.[4]

Up till the 1970s, most of the available information in the West about Daqing came from a report written by someone intimate to the oil industry who later became a mainland refugee and escaped to Taiwan.[5] In his report, this unnamed refugee indicated to the Taiwanese authorities that Daqing was first surveyed in 1956 while another source in Hong Kong mentioned that the oilfield was aerially surveyed.[6] Daqing's name is derived from a combination of the word "Da (Big)" in Dawahong (Tawahung) and "Qing (Celebration)" in Qingan (Chingan), the two geographical markers lying 48 degrees north and 128 degrees east that are used to delineate Daqing.[7] Daqing's name was as enigmatic as the oilfield during the days of PRC's information non-disclosure in the oil industry. Other accounts, including Lieberthal and IDE-JETRO argue that it was the coincidence of Daqing's discovery with the 10th anniversary of the PRC's founding that gave rise to the name Daqing which also means Great Celebration.[8]

ORIGINS

According to Japan's Institute of Development Economies, Daqing's oil potential was first broached when Mao Zedong asked prominent geologist Li Siguang the million dollar question of where oil can be found in China.[9] Li replied that, within all of China's lands (*zhongguo quantu*), one should mine for oil at the Northeast for rich deposits of oil.[10] Though the exact date of the statement was not

[4] Park, C. (1975). *Energy Policies of the World: China*, p. 14. Newark Delaware: Center for the Study of Marine Policy.

[5] Chan L.W. (1974). *The Taching Oilfield A Maoist Model for Economic Development Contemporary China Papers No. 8*, p. 8. Australia: Australian National University Press.

[6] Ibid.

[7] Bartke, W. (1977), p. 70.

[8] Tatsu, K. (2002), p. 16.

[9] Ibid., p. 14.

[10] Ibid., pp. 14-15.

known, it was said to have narrowed down China's search considerably by concentrating resources in a particular region that eventually made the discovery of Daqing possible. The actual work was much more complicated and integrates intrigue, politics, ideological battles and concepts of self-reliance.

THE PETROLEUM FACTION

The officials who developed the Daqing oilfield in the early 1960s, largely the same group whom Mao assembled in 1964–5 to run the economy, became known in China as the "Petroleum Faction" (*shiyou pai*) headed by Yu Qiuli. The Petroleum Faction originally started the development of the Daqing oil field under Yu Qiuli between 1964 to 1966 as a new planning commission.[11] Centered around Yu Qiuli and including Kang Shien and Tang Ke, its members controlled the energy sector and headed several principal economic agencies in China by the early 1970s. In the early 1960s, the Petroleum Faction appeared committed to the virtues of self-reliance and mobilizational techniques for policy implementation by the early 1970s, but they modified their views as opportunities and requirements had changed. When China was re-integrated back into the international community after the Nixon rapprochement, the Petroleum Faction became proponents of importing technology and exporting petroleum to hasten economic development.

The newness of the Petroleum Faction, Daqing's rapid growth and a dispersion of the Faction's leaders and technicians from Daqing to other government organizations gave the Faction and its host, the Ministry of Petroleum Industry (MPI) a legendary reputation. Its progressive outlook and excellent track record also ensured that the PRC petroleum bureaucracy was less plagued by deeply-rooted groupings and cleavages found in other ministries.[12] They were bound together and they prospered and suffered together. They were the patrons of larger networks of individuals within MPI (Ministry of Petroleum Industry)

[11] Lieberthal, K. and Oksenberg, M. (1986), p. 22.

[12] Ibid., p. 65.

and other agencies who looked to them for protection, advancement and rewards. They were clearly bonded by personal ties rooted in much more than common policy preferences and transitional bureaucratic responsibilities. The Petroleum Faction also had loyal allies and former subordinates located at various levels in the State Planning Commission (SPC); State Economic Commission (SEC); the Ministry of Finance, coal chemical and metallurgy industries, as well as in the State Council.

THE DISCOVERY OF DAQING

Between 1956–1959, the Northeast Petroleum Exploration Brigade of the Ministry of Geology, the Songliao Petroleum Exploration Bureau of the Ministry of Petroleum and the Songliao Petroleum Investigation Brigade of the Jilin Provincial Bureau of Petroleum jointly conducted a comprehensive survey of the swampy, mosquito-infested grasslands of the Songliao plain, a region in Manchuria in the western portions of Heilongjiang and Jilin provinces.[13] The conceptual foundation for this frenzied search was to hit upon something momentous to propel China into oil self-reliance, in line with their inherited Russian philosophy of "shoot for the elephants and ignore the mice".[14]

Some accounts viewed the process as technological exploration. IDE-JETRO's study on oil noted the use of magnetometer mounted on aircraft for oil searches.[15] Such accounts corroborate official contemporary versions of Chinese oil industry history written by the oil industry press (*Shiyou Gongye Chubanshe*) in the PRC. According to Yang Jiliang's essay *Daqing Youtian de Faxian Guocheng* (*The Chronology of the Discovery of the Daqing Oilfield*) published in *Dangdai Zhongguo Youqi Kantan Zhongda Faxian* (*The Important Discoveries of Contemporary China's Oil and Gas Exploration*) in 1999, the exploration teams deployed to Daqing consisted of nine magnetometer teams, armed with drills that were able to hit 3,200 m and 1,000 m as well as one consolidated research team

[13] Ibid., p. 154.

[14] Cheng, C. (1976). *China's Petroleum Industry,* p. 3. New York: Praeger.

[15] Tatsu, K. (2002), p. 15.

specializing in physics, another with expertise in monitoring formations and two other oil-well electronic assessment teams.[16] A high-ranking bureau chief (Li Xinghe) and his deputy (Song Shikuan) from the oil industry department's Songliao oil exploration bureau based in Changchun city were deployed along with these teams for the exploration expeditions.[17]

Initial results appeared to be most promising and an exploration plan was quickly drawn up. On 8 May 1959, *Renmin Ribao* (*People's Daily*) published an article that would prove to have great consequences for the Chinese oil industry.[18] In that article, it was reported that the Ministry of Petroleum and the Ministry of Geology had decided to give highest priority to exploration for oil in the Songliao plain. Testing and evaluation of oil potential in that area were concentrated in the most promising areas of the plain.

Activities at these sites were intense and furious. Guerilla tactics adapted from warfare were applied at this stage. According to Japan's Ministry of Foreign Affairs, the two guerrilla tactics of choice were "*Huizhan Zhihuibu*" (Command Post for a Great Battle) and "*Dichanmie Zhanzhen*" (The War for Total Elimination of the Enemy).[19] The association of Daqing with these guerilla tactics is so prevalent that the *New Century Chinese-English Dictionary* approved by the Foreign Language Teaching and Research Press uses Daqing as an example to elaborate on the meaning of the Chinese word "*huizhan*".[20]

---

[16] Yang, J. (1999). Daqing Youtian de Faxian Guocheng (The Chronology of the Discovery of the Daqing Oilfield). In *Dangdai Zhongguo Youqi Kantan Zhongda Faxian (The Important Discoveries of Contemporary China's Oil and Gas Exploration)*, Zhang, W. ed. p. 277. Beijing: Shiyou Gongye Chubanshe.

[17] Ibid.

[18] Lieberthal, K. and Oksenberg, M. (1986), p. 154.

[19] Gaimusho Keizaikyoku Keizaitogoka (Japan's Ministry of Foreign Affairs Economics Bureau Economics Statistics Section) (1970). *Chugoku Tariku no Shigen to Chukyo no Shigen Seisaku (Mainland China's Resources and Chinese Communist Party's Resource Policies)*, p. 168.

[20] Foreign Language Teaching and Research Press (2002). *New Century Chinese-English Dictionary*, p. 532. Singapore: Foreign Language Teaching and Research Press and Learners Publishing.

Both doctrines focused on an overwhelming concentration of power on a point of attack. Following these doctrines, PRC exploration personnel converged upon the Songliao plain from points in Xinjiang and the Beijing Petroleum Research Institute (also translated as Beijing Petrochemical Institute by some writers[21]) while a large amount of exploration and drilling equipment were airlifted and surface-transported to the work site.[22] Airlifting of equipment was expensive and rarely utilized in China in the late 1950s.[23] Its use in Songliao thus highlighted the importance which the government had attached to this effort.

To overcome inadequacies in equipment, trained manpower and funding, China adopted the strategy of concentrating its entire national resources, which was considerable at 170,000 workers, over 1 billion Chinese yuan and over 100 drilling machines, on a few well-selected prioritized tasks under the direct regimented military-like leadership of the Ministry of Petroleum's Yu Qiuli and his deputies like Kang Shien and Sun Jingwen.[24] Through sheer numbers, industries previously set up with Soviet help and requiring the presence of Soviet technicians began to find their own ways of producing the same machinery when the Soviet advisors were withdrawn.

The organization formed to search for the oilfield that would eventually become Daqing was run like a secret military operation. Daqing's exploratory organization mobilized rural manpower for its operations and were organized into military units.The command post and headquarters of the prospecting operations was codenamed "*nongken zhongchang* (the head farm)".[25] Subordinate sub-units codenamed "*fenchang* (branch farm)" and each *fenchang* had its own postal code (*xinxiang*) while the command post had the postal code "101 xinxiang".[26] In the command post, not even Secretary General

---

[21] Lee,T. H. (1995), p. 113.

[22] Lieberthal, K. and Oksenberg, M. (1986), p. 155.

[23] Ibid.

[24] Wen, *et al.* (2002), pp. 100–101.

[25] Chen, D. K. (1994), p. 125.

[26] Ibid.

Liu Haisheng could tell his young wife at home the location of his office and workplace.[27]

Zhongguo Shiyou Dahui Zhan (*A Chinese Great Battle for Oil*) published by the military press Bayi Chubanshe described the cordial civilian-military camaraderie at Daqing: "When the technicians and the professional soldiers came, the peasants behaved as during the war years in welcoming their team members into their mud huts, turning up the bonfires with several generations of men, women, seniors and youngsters huddling up with the oil workers in the same huts around the same bonfires (*Huizhande gongrenmen laile, zhuanyede jiefangjun laile. Nongminmen yiran xiang zhanzheng niandai nayang, bazhijide duiwu yingjin jianloude tuwu, batukeng shaode rerede, nannu laishao jibeiren he shiyou zhanshi jizai yiwuli, yikengshang*)".[28]

Railroads (such as the one from Harbin to Qiqihar) as well as railway depots like Anda were cleared for clear lines of communication and transportation for this project.[29] In 1958, a test well which was drilled in April was found to contain oil and this became a push factor for 30 more exploratory wells to be dug within the same year.[30] Between 9 July to 1 November 1958, in the Northeast slopes of the Songliao basin, a team from the Songliao Exploratory Bureau (*Songliao Kantanju*) drilled a 1,879 m deep hole, Songji No. 1, 14 miles south of Anda County, Renmin Town but found no oil.[31] In August that year, in the autonomous ethnic Mongolian county of Kuoerluoshi, Songji No. 2 was dug but again showed little promise of oil.[32] Due to the dismal outcome of these two digs, the third dig became an object of intense contention and debate and was only resolved in September 1958, when the Ministries of Geology and Petroleum reached a settlement on the location of Songji No. 3.[33]

---

[27] Ibid.

[28] Chen, D. K. (1994), p. 127.

[29] Lieberthal, K. and Oksenberg, M. (1986), p. 155.

[30] Ling, H. C. (1975), p. 127.

[31] Wen, *et al.* (2002), p. 88.

[32] Wen, *et al.* (2002), pp. 88–89.

[33] Wen, *et al.* (2002), pp. 97–98.

On 9 September 1959, MPI struck oil in Songji No. 3 in the Songliao plain.[34] Seventeen days later, on 26 September, test oil well No. 3 gushed with commercially viable supplies of oil.[35] By 1960, Daqing operators had mapped out the area (estimated 20 by 50 km) and estimated its reserves (about 85.5 to 120 million metric tons).[36] In the following months, the Chinese drilled 22 test wells and evaluated the boundaries of the oil field, discovering that the area actually covered 200 square kilometers and that it consisted of a total of seven oilfields.[37] Fortunately, the oil wells were shallow averaging only 1,000 meters in depth, needing only two weeks to work on each of them.[38]

Songji No. 3 was located in Datong Town and, to avoid confusing Datong's oil well with the famous Datong Coal Mine in Shanxi, recommendation was made for its name to be changed.[39] The site was given a name that reflected the euphoria which struck the nation. It was called Daqing (Great Celebration), an auspicious name chosen out of recognition that the discovery occurred on the eve of the widely celebrated 10th anniversary of the founding of the PRC. This good news soon reached the Chinese leadership in Zhongnanhai in Beijing and received prominent mention during the National Day celebrations.

Vice-Minister of Geology, Ho Changgong, had Daqing in mind when he wrote his *Renmin Ribao* article of 11 October 1959: "In the Great Leap Forward, we greatly strengthened work in the Northeast, especially in the discovery of oil in the Songliao area. The discovery of this oilfield will be very important for the development of our country's petroleum industry."[40] The paramount importance of the discovery at Daqing was underlined by the fact that Premier Zhou Enlai personally departed for Harbin to gather personnel from the

---

[34] Wen, *et al.* (2002), p. 98.
[35] Lieberthal, K. and Oksenberg, M. (1986), p. 155.
[36] Chan, L.W. (1974), p. 9.
[37] Lieberthal, K. and Oksenberg, M. (1986), p. 156.
[38] Chan, L.W. (1974), p. 9.
[39] Wen, *et al.* (2002), p. 98.
[40] Lieberthal, K. and Oksenberg, M. (1986), p. 156.

MPI and the Heilongjiang Party committee to make concrete plans for extraction.[41] The discovery also brought entire sub-bureaus of ministries and state commissions to the provincial capitals of the region where oil was discovered, including Heilongjiang.[42] Anda (An-ta in Wades Giles), the nearest town to Daqing was raised from a *xian* (*hsien* or county) to city status.[43]

Drilling of the first large productive oil well was completed on 14 April 1960 and, almost instantaneously, the first shipment of crude petroleum left Daqing by rail in June 1960, less than two months later.[44] Other than the fact that this perhaps represented China's first significant shipment of oil drawn from its own resources, the drills used also made news as they were made entirely by the Chinese themselves in factories located in Xi'an, Zhangjiakou, Kunming and various industries.[45] The first year of the Daqing project was predominantly devoted to a more precise evaluation and delineation of the geographic size, geological composition and reserve potential of the Daqing area and, in the following three years from 1961 to 1963, production went full steam ahead.[46]

The work on Daqing did not lose momentum in its early years. It continually received visits by high level leaders who were also its patrons, like Liu Shaoqi and Deng Xiaoping on August 9, 1961. Premier Zhou Enlai was a repeat visitor who went to Daqing in 1962 and again in 1963. Zhou's June 1962 tour of Daqing was personally guided by Yu Qiuli where Zhou repeatedly stopped to talk to the workers at the ground level.[47] Even Mao's wife, Jiang Qing, who would come into prominence during the Cultural Revolution a few

---

[41] Ibid. p. 157.

[42] Spence, J. (1999). *The Search for Modern China*, p. 659. NY and London: WW Norton and Company.

[43] Chan, L.W. (1974), p. 8.

[44] Lieberthal, K. and Oksenberg, M. (1986), p. 157.

[45] Gaimusho Keizaikyoku Keizaitogoka (Japan's Ministry of Foreign Affairs Economics Bureau Economics Statistics Section) (1970), p. 168.

[46] Lieberthal, K. and Oksenberg, M. (1986), p. 157.

[47] Yu, Q. (1996). *Yu Qiuli Huiyilu (Memoirs of Yu Qiuli)*. Beijing: Jiefangjun Chubanshe (The PLA Press).

years later, reportedly visited the field in 1961 and witnessed the dedication of individual wells to the Chairman, Premier Zhou, and Liu Shaoqi.[48] The gaze of the elite continually fell upon the sacrifice and pathos of the nation's most productive oil wells. In a strange twist of fate, some of these visitors would become diabolical denouncers of Daqing during the Cultural Revolution while others would be its guardians to tide through the same difficult period.

Production rose quickly in Daqing from 1960 to 1963. According to the *Peking Review* in its edition of January 3, 1975, the annual increase in Daqing's crude oil production since 1960 was 31 percent.[49] While this figure might have been an exaggeration, the trend of increased production was real and authentic. Even more significantly, with the peaking of the old Yumen field during this period and the reduction in imports from the Soviet Union, the role of Daqing in China's overall oil industry had become crucial by the end of 1963. Figures coming out of Daqing were dazzling (See Table 2.1). As a percentage of the total availability of petroleum in China (domestic production and imports), Daqing's share rose from roughly nine percent to an incredible 46 percent in 1963.[50] As a percentage of China's domestic crude production, Daqing rose from 15 percent in 1960 to 19 percent in 1961, 47 percent in 1962 and 68 percent in 1963.[51]

CHINESE OIL INSTITUTIONS

Within the PRC centralized planning system, a specialized division was delegated the technical task of managing and exploiting oil resources. As the Bureau of Petroleum[52] grew, it needed greater resources and the PRC's Ministry of Petroleum Industry (sometimes

[48] Lieberthal, K. and Oksenberg, M. (1986), p. 157.

[49] Bernardo, R. M. (1977). *Popular Management and Pay in China,* p. 178. Quezon City, Philippines: University of the Philippines Press.

[50] Lieberthal, K. and Oksenberg, M. (1986), p. 157.

[51] Ibid.

[52] Ling, H. C. (1975), p. 49.

Table 2.1: Daqing's role in the national petroleum supply. Availability of Crude Petroleum and Petroleum Products, 1960–1963 (Million Metric Tons)

	1	2	3	4	5	6
1960	5.20	2.96	0.91	9.07	0.79	8.70
1961	5.31	2.93	0.46	8.70	(1.02)	12.7
1962	5.75	1.86	1.14	8.75	(2.73)	31.2
1963	6.48	1.41	1.60	9.49	4.40	46.3

1. Domestic Crude Petroleum Production
2. Petroleum imports from USSR
3. Imports from other countries
4. Total petroleum supply
5. Daqing production
6. % of total supply

Source: Lieberthal, K. and Oksenberg, M. (1986). *Bureaucratic Politics and Chinese Energy Development*, p. 159. Prepared for the Department of Commerce Contract No. 50-SATA-4-16230), Washington: Center for Chinese Studies, The University of Michigan.
Notes: Column 1 is derived from State Statistical Bureau (ed.) (1983). *Zhongguo tongji nianjian* (*China Statistical Yearbook*), p. 245. Beijing: Chinese Statistical Press. Columns 2, 3 and 5 are from Barnett, A. D. (1981). *China's Economy in Global Perspective*, pp. 436–437, 459. Washington: The Bookings Institution. The Daqing estimates originate with the CIA. (See CIA (1977). *China: Oil Production Prospects*, ER 77-100 OU, p. 9). These CIA estimates merit confidence, since the CIA estimates of total production have proven to be remarkably close to subsequent Chinese disclosures. The CIA series is within 2% of the Chinese production figure for each year from 1960 through 1963. Column 4 is the sum of Columns 1, 2 and 3. It is not clear that these columns should be aggregated, in that Columns 2 and 3 refer to both crude petroleum and petroleum products, while Column 1 refers to crude petroleum production. Clearly, a ton of petroleum products is derived from more than a ton of crude petroleum, and it is not clear whether Columns 2 and 3 simply add crude and products or whether the product is adjusted to a crude equivalent. This problem with the data, however, does not detract from the basic conclusion which the table yields.

translated as Petroleum Ministry or Ministry of Petroleum in various publications) was set up in July 1955.[53] The full-fledged ministry dedicated to petroleum that grew out of the reorganization of Ministry of Fuel Industry reflected PRC's concern with oil development.

[53] Bartke, W. (1977), p. 49; Cheng, C. (1976), p. 3; and Ling, H. C. (1975), p. 49.

MPI was an elite institution.Those working in PRC's Daqing under the MPI were called "*Daqingren* (the people of Daqing)". Daqing and MPI were thought to be some of the choicest places to work in the PRC, attracting the best and the brightest. As an expanding organization, it offered opportunities for mobility that other agencies lacked. Furthermore, since wages were held constant in the PRC, the distinguishing marks of an elite organization were the perks and better services enjoyed by its members.

Petroleum bureaucrats in Beijing, for example, secured housing facilities from the MPI and enjoyed shower facilities at their workplace as well as state provision of meals in the canteen at the Ministry. MPI also gave out perks and access to scarce commodities like television sets and theater tickets.[54] In 1969, owning a TV set required 165-425 days' worth of an average worker's pay.[55] Perks for MPI's employees was all made possible because Daqing under the MPI was earning considerable revenue for the state and, consequently, MPI was able to retain a portion of its revenue to provide better services for its employees both in Beijing and outside.

MPI's centralized powers persisted and even intensified from when Daqing was discovered right through to Deng's era. In the report that Kenneth Lieberthal submitted to the US Department of Commerce in August 1986, he described MPI as: "Compared to most other ministries, MPI is highly centralized. At its headquarters, it has the usual staff bureaus of finance, foreign affairs planning, capital construction, personnel, education, and science and technology which have liaison with the relevant commissions and ministries. It also has such operative bureaus such as transportation and marketing, supplies, drilling and engineering equipment manufacturing, oilfield development, and geological exploration. These bureaus directly lead subordinate units in various oil and natural gas fields."[56] After the

[54] Lieberthal, K. and Oksenberg, M. (1986), p. 65.

[55] Richman, B. M. (1969). *Industrial Society in Communist China*, p. 808. New York: Vintage Books.

[56] Lieberthal, K. and Oksenberg, M. (1986), p. 68.

Cultural Revolution, the Chinese government encouraged the merger of Ministry of Petroleum Industry, Ministry of Coal Industry and Ministry of Chemical Industry into the Ministry of Fuel and Chemical Industry.[57] On the eve of China's market liberalization in 1979, another change took place and the renamed Ministry of Petroleum was in firm control of oil production with only powers devolved in the areas of oil refining split between itself and a few other ministries.[58]

The MPI was extremely successful in the pre-reform phase of the PRC economy. The Ministry raised the production of petroleum from 5.2 MMT in 1960 to 104.1 MMT in 1978.[59] The Ministry also converted China from a net oil importer into an exporter with Daqing accounting for over 50 percent of the production (1960–1984) and contributed profits of 68.1 billion RMB between 1960 to 1984 to the state.[60] This figure was approximately 20 times the value of capital investments by the state in Daqing and no less than three percent of state revenue (from all enterprise profits and taxes) comes from Daqing.[61] In 1960, China expended $150–175 million (10 percent of its foreign expenditures on petroleum importation) but, in 1978, it exported 13.6 MMT of petroleum and its associated products, drawing in US$1.3 billion or 11 percent of its foreign exchange earnings with the figure rising to 29 MMT, US$6.4 billion or 23 percent of its foreign earnings.[62]

Aside from governmental agency and ministerial level institutions, the PRC developed its own self-contained regional production centers. The Daqing Oil Field Administration Bureau had far more sophisticated functional units, 67 in five sectors dealing with core oil businesses, service companies, public infrastructure, diversified businesses

---

[57] Ling, H. C. (1975), pp. 6 and 49.

[58] Horsnell, P. (1997). *Oil in Asia*, p. 41. UK: Oxford University Press for the Oxford Institution for Energy Studies.

[59] Lieberthal, K. and Oksenberg, M. (1986), p. 64.

[60] Ibid.

[61] Lieberthal, K. and Oksenberg, M. (1986), p. 65.

[62] Ibid.

and social functions.[63] The conceptualization behind this organizational structure, *da er quan* (big and comprehensive),[64] stressed on isolating themselves from interactions with small local factories and enterprises,[65] thus restricting their dependence on external sub-contracting firms at the same time. They were firmly put under central planning and shielded from outside help. The Daqing municipality and petroleum industry were centralized under one administration which takes charge of oil production, agriculture, services, public security and civilian affairs.[66]

Daqing was run as a self-contained city or military-industrial complex. It also reflected one of the basic features of corporatism in that constituent units are organized into a limited number of singular, non-competitive, hierarchically-ordered and functionally-differentiated categories which were granted autonomy within their units.[67] The innovation in Daqing is the self-contained sub-unit. The main self-contained system (*da er quan*) envelopes smaller self-contained units (*xiao er quan* or small and comprehensive) like the No. 1 Oil Extracting Plant with its 30 brigades in five sectors covering similar functions as the main system but on a smaller scale.[68] These complex organisms very much reflected the modernization goals in heavy industries with massive production outputs in an attempt to leapfrog and join the developed world.

The Communist Party sought to integrate specialists into the party ranks. This system was proposed by Yu Qiuli, the pioneer and leader of Daqing, in 1960[69] with three main characteristics. First, academics and

---

[63] Zhang, J. (2004). *Catch-up and Competitiveness in China*, p. 75. London and New York: RoutledgeCurzon.

[64] Ibid., p. 76.

[65] Rawski, T. G. (1980). *China's Transition to Industrialism*, p. 24. Ann Arbor: The University of Michigan Press.

[66] Bartke, W. (1977), p. 75.

[67] Schmitter, P. C. Still the Century of Corporatism? In *Modernity Critical Concepts Volume III Modern Systems*, Waters, M. (ed.). p. 477. London and New York: Routledge.

[68] Zhang, J. (2004), p. 76.

[69] Chen, D. K. (1994), p. 146.

theoreticians with oilfield expertise would be deployed to the field[70] (partly reflecting Yu's distrust of the intellectuals) to prevent armchair theocracy from forming that may challenge the Party or field units' initiatives and directives. Second, spot and select young talents to understudy and succeed their senior counterparts in the field.[71] And, third, these promising young talents as well as other technicians were then integrated into Party organs at every level of the organizational hierarchy so that the Party is able to efficiently and quickly absorb crucial operatives of the oilfield.[72]

Yu was determined to reverse the situation of Party committees comprising of technocrats as the minority through promoting and cultivating batches of technically-trained Party members with a few years of experience at Songliao.[73] In concert with these plans, within three and a half years of surveying and exploiting Daqing, eight were promoted to become head engineers, 63 to supervising engineers, 307 to the position of engineer (including exploitation, drilling, geological engineers) with most of them hovering around the age of 30.[74] In total, 1,574 personnel were promoted to positions of leadership (including the non-engineering posts).[75]

WELFARISM

When Daqing first started out as an oil-prospecting project, it had the barest of living conditions for the workers. Some of these conditions were naturally imposed by the weather and climatic conditions at the Songliao plains but others were imposed deliberately by its leaders. Daqing was symbolized by its harsh climatic condition and lack of food for workers, especially fresh vegetables, something that only changed later with man-made improvements to soil condition and

[70] Ibid., p. 151.
[71] Ibid.
[72] Ibid.
[73] Ibid., p. 152.
[74] Ibid., p. 151.
[75] Ibid.

irrigation.[76] In terms of amenities, in its early days, Daqing did not have any toilet or sofas and other "luxurious items (*shechipin*)" despite being allocated substantial sums of money by the central government, for e.g., Deng Xiaoping once authorized 200 million yuan as the head of the petroleum industry party committee (*Shiyou Gongyebu Dangzhu*) for Daqing operations.[77]

Some of Daqing's sparse facilities were self-imposed.The frugality practiced during the early Daqing days was initiated by its commanding officer,Yu Qiuli, who laid down three golden rules to optimize the use of limited funds: the first rule was that the purchase of vehicles was disallowed; the second was the ban on commanding units procuring sofas, carpets and other commercial products; and the third was prohibiting solitary accommodations.[78]

Leslie Chan's explanation for Yu's frugality was that he needed to use funds strictly only for oil production, given the high pressures he faced in looking for oil within China's space. Yu was not able to use the limited funds for other purposes and thus workers and their dependents had to make do with the best they could find.[79] There were not even enough funds to buy tractors for farming even though Daqing instituted a self-dependence policy for workers to grow everything they consumed. Chan noted that the increase of personal savings deposited in Daqing banks from 40,000 yuan in 1964 to 260,000 yuan in July 1966 was enough to cover expenditures like the tractors.[80]

Yu's legendary frugality extended even to his dealings with his subordinates at Daqing. He once chastized model oil worker Ironman Wang Jinxi for buying a West German-made scooter which he criticized as a "*yangjiahuo* (Western-made thing)" — a mildly derisive term for foreign-made goods.[81] Wang had to persuade Yu that his

---

[76] Liu, M. (1979). *Laojunmiao de Gushi* (*The Story of Laojunmiao*), p. 46. Taipei: Huaqiao Wenhua Chubanshe.

[77] Chen, D. K. (1994), p. 128.

[78] Ibid.

[79] Chan, L.W. (1974), p. 16.

[80] Ibid.

[81] Chen, D. K. (1994), p. 136.

scooter was purchased with his own borrowed funds for use at the oilfield to speed up his travels between oil wells or to transport tools.[82] With great difficulty, Wang finally won over Yu who ended his criticism and asked Wang to observe traffic safety.[83]

But conditions improved once oil was a proven asset at Daqing. One million square meters were set aside for the project as two to three-roomed housing for its workers between 1963–1965 and in 1964, with the goal of self-reliance in mind, several million jin (1 jin = 650 g) of grains like wheat and soya beans as well as vegetables were harvested and 15,000 pigs and other animals raised in the vicinity.[84] On 2 January 1973, the Chinese authorities reported through the New China News Agency (Xinhua) that Daqing produced 25,000 tons of grain and 30,000 tons of vegetables annually in an article entitled *New Type Socialist Oilfield — Fourth in a Series on Taching*.[85]

The article also mentioned: "Not far from the administration building is a village with well over 1,300 households and 5,500 members of workers' families. The village has production teams working 466 hectares of farmland".[86] This was a significant achievement as Daqing's lands were described as "*mujin no kouya* (no man's land)"[87] by foreign observers. Wasteland was cultivated with wheat and soya beans grown and, in a unique farm, 1,000 staff members tended to the raising of deer while achieving self-reliance in vegetable cultivation Daqing.[88]

Daqing's relatively flat land and nutrient rich soil were suitable for wheat, soya beans, sugar beet and flax.[89] The families of the operators in Daqing altogether cultivated 33,000 acres and produced over 20,000 tons of grain and 15,000 tons of vegetables, in addition to rearing

---

[82] Ibid., pp. 135 and 139.

[83] Chen, D. K. (1994), pp. 139–140.

[84] Bartke, W. (1977), p. 74.

[85] Cheng, C. (1976), p. 13; and Ling, H. C. (1975), p. 235.

[86] Ling, H. C. (1975), p. 235.

[87] Tatsu, K. (2002), p. 17.

[88] Bartke, W. (1977), p. 75.

[89] Chan, L. W. (1974), p. 10.

horses, donkeys, cattle, pigs, sheep, poultry and fishes.[90] Oilwells and cornfields lie side by side.[91] Grasslands were given the utmost attention to preserve their soil condition.[92] In order not to disturb the crops, Daqing operations such as laying more than 200,000 tons of pipes and moving 14 million tons of earth and rock in constructing these pipelines were carried out in winter to prevent damage to crops since agriculture is at its ebb during the winter season.[93]

Amenities. In Daqing, social welfare was also well-taken care of with a 50-bed hospital, a middle school for 1,500 children with a nine-year curriculum and natural gas supplied for heating and cooking.[94] In 1972, an additional psychiatric hospital was set up in Daqing with 400 mattresses, five wards and space for 200 beds.[95] Workers were also secure with lifetime employment and a cradle to grave welfare system.[96] According to Wolfgang Bartke, in 1966 all residential quarters in Taching (Daqing) had schools, nurseries, dining halls and shops.

Daqing continued the tradition of state-managed educational facilities at oilfield facilities. In the central districts there were hospitals, middle schools, department stores, post offices, hairdressers' and tailors' shop, and tractor stations, as well as official buildings with large halls for conferences or film and theatre performances. In addition to the primary schools, there were 16 secondary schools, combining study and practical work, where students could specialize in geology, oil drilling techniques, agricultural machinery, education, finance

[90] Ibid., p. 11.
[91] Bartke, W. (1977), p. 75.
[92] Cheng, C. (1976), p. 11.
[93] Bartke, W. (1977), p. 73.
[94] Ibid., p. 75.
[95] Zhonggong Daqing Youtian Disan Yiyuan Weiyuanhui (The Chinese Communist Party Daqing Oilfield No. 3 Hospital Committee) (1977). Shenru Kaizhan Weisheng Geming Yong Daqing Jingshen Ban Yiyuan (To Thoroughly Launch a Revolution in Health Using the Daqing Spirit to Manage a Hospital). In *Gongye Zhanxian de Xianyan Hongqi* (*The Brightly-Colored Red Flag of the Industrial Battlefront*), p. 294. China: Renminchubanshe.
[96] Zhang, J. (2004), p. 139.

or medicine. In addition an Institute of Petrochemistry has been established."[97] Gathering from this, one could assume that life at Daqing in many ways was better than other parts of China. In 1966, a decision was made to move the Beijing Petroleum College[98] and Beijing Petrochemical Institute[99] to Daqing as a concerted effort to make Daqing a training nucleus for the oil industry.

A wide network of roads connected various hamlets with each other, with urbanization transcending the wide industrial and agricultural space; Wolfgang Bartke described it as giving "the region an appearance that is at once urban and rural".[100] He added further that "industry and agriculture, town and countryside are integrated".[101] One thousand four hundred workers and their families live in the central hamlet known as the "Red Satellite" settlement covering 30 square kilometers[102] and consisting of five villages at a distance of between one to 1.5 km apart.[103] Depending on the number of family members, each household has two or three rooms allocated to them.[104] Cheng Chu-yuan describes a slightly different configuration in his 1976 publication *China's Petroleum Industry*. He observed that "400,000 inhabitants were drawn from all parts of the nation and were resettled in 40 townships scattered over the region with urban facilities at the center, each township being linked with two or three satellite village residential areas."[105]

In 1977, in the years of China's re-opening to the outside world, the "Red Satellite" settlement was described as having a grain shop, a department store, a group of tailors, a bookshop, a post office, a photographic studio, a public bath, a radio repair shop and a kindergarten for children between the ages of two months and seven years.[106]

---

[97] Bartke, W. (1977), p. 75.
[98] Park, C. (1975), p. 14.
[99] Lee, T. H. (1995), p. 113.
[100] Bartke, W. (1977), p. 75.
[101] Ibid.
[102] Ibid., p. 76.
[103] Ibid., p. 75.
[104] Ibid.
[105] Cheng, C. (1976), p. 11.
[106] Bartke, W. (1977), p. 75.

For the workers' culinary needs, there was also a food-processing plant, a distillery, a factory making soya bean curd and soya sauce and a dining hall for the workers.[107] Like Beijing oil bureaucrats with their elitist status and perks of TVs and theater tickets as well as their higher than average salary at 287 yuan,[108] Daqing workers developed an esprit de corps of their own, even having their own nomenclature of "Daqing people (Daqing *ren*)".[109] There were also many free services for the Daqing community such as provision of electricity, gas, water, intra-complex bus travel, barbers and bath houses.[110] The tremendous pride of being part of Daqing made it easier later for the facility to develop a corporate identity in the era of gradual privatization.

Public welfare, however, was not unproblematic. The Communist Party Committee of Daqing's psychiatric hospital admitted that running a facility like this carried some ideological risks because of the medical field's association with capitalist tendencies and class stratification. In one case, a doctor was found guilty of privately selling prescription drugs from 1973 onwards, scamming terminally-ill patients and illegally selling drugs from the hospital to village medical units at a high price.[111] A hospital driver was found guilty stealing vehicle spare parts and stealing 100 tools of various kinds.[112] Both were used as negative examples of class conflicts.

In countering these bad apples, hospital staff who were selfless, however, were designated model workers when they returned gifts from the families of patients, stressing that their work was for the betterment of society and gratitude should be attributed to the Communist Party, Mao and socialism instead of individual staff members.[113] Patients and their families were urged to discard their old feudal ways

[107] Ibid.

[108] Chan, L.W. (1974), p. 15.

[109] Zhang, J. (2004), p. 139.

[110] Chan, L.W. (1974), p. 15.

[111] Zhonggong Daqing Youtian Disan Yiyuan Weiyuanhui (The Chinese Communist Party Daqing Oilfield No. 3 Hospital Committee) (1977), pp. 294–295.

[112] Ibid., p. 295.

[113] Ibid., p. 297.

of thinking and do battle with the bourgeoisie mentality. According to Daqing literature, they were praised by the peasantry for these acts of selflessness.

Testimonies given by hospital staff were just as ideologically fertile. One female patient apparently was sold without her knowledge to a family which made her carry out laborious tasks in pre-1949 China.[114] Mao and the Communist Party rescued her from her misery but, for some unknown reasons, she ended up in Daqing with mental illness. After numerous injections and electro-therapy, the patient remained unresponsive. The hospital then engaged her brother to give testimonies which dwelled on her past life, triggering off the "incomparable love (*wubireai*)"[115] of socialism to inspire staff members to organize themselves into four teams to tend to this patient continuously. Miraculously, she gradually recovered and was able to manage some functions of her own, including eating and toilet skills.[116]

This story was not unique as other accounts of socialism having positive effects on mental ailments were recorded in Daqing literature. To boost the fighting spirit of some of these patients, hospital staff members even sat by them to read to them from Mao's works and unravel his guidance.[117] In accordance with these testimonies, the immense power of Mao's thoughts (*Mao Zedong shixiang weilida*) was also responsible for keeping the behavior of mental patients in check when they were brought out in public for excursions to Harbin.[118]

DAQING COMES OF AGE

With the discovery and development of Daqing between 1959 to 1963, the oil industry came into its own and had its own Minister of

---

[114] Ibid.

[115] Ibid., p. 298.

[116] Ibid.

[117] Ibid., p. 299.

[118] Ibid., p. 301.

Petroleum, Yu Qiuli. Also known as the "one-arm general *(dubi jiangjun)*",[119] he was a Long March veteran and seasoned soldier. He personally supervised the work at Daqing during the winter of 1959–1960 with other pioneers of the project like Kang Shien, Tang Ke and Song Zhenming. Their political acumen was complemented with the support of several extremely capable engineers who guided technical activities in the 1960s and 1970s.

To process crude oil at Daqing, a modern refinery was first constructed in April 1962 (completed one year later)[120] with a designated annual capacity of one million tons with continual upgrades doubling its output to 2.5 million tons in 1971 and five million tons in 1974 according to Western sources published in the 1970s.[121] According to oil historiography, the Daqing refinery was first approved by the national planning and construction commission committee *(Guojia Jiwei he Jianwei)* in December 1960 with the first phase targeted at an output of 100 tons per year.[122] It was a hurried job with the initial stage of the first phase completed in the first half of 1961 but faced many challenges including the difficulties of refining waxy and coagulative Daqing crude.[123]

On 6 November 1963, PRC's first self-designed, self-constructed and indigenous large-scale refinery with compression function was completed, thus overcoming another step in its quest to become self-reliant in oil energy.[124] In terms of actual output, by 1963, Daqing churned out 4.4 million metric tons of oil, over two-third of China's total output.[125] On a per day basis, Daqing was churning out 85,000 barrels of oil per day by 1965.[126] In 1965, an oil refinery was constructed

---

[119] Chen, D. K. (1994), p. 300. Chinese oil literature does not specify how he lost the use of his right arm.

[120] Cheng, C. (1976), p. 59.

[121] Ibid.

[122] Wen, *et al.* (2002), p. 143.

[123] Ibid.

[124] Ibid., p. 146.

[125] Spence, J. (1999). *The Search for Modern China*, p. 563. NY and London, WW Norton and Company.

[126] Horsnell, P. (1997), p. 47.

in lightning time of only a year and a half of construction.[127] In 1966, its refining capacity more than doubled from one to 2.5 million tons annually.[128] Between 1960 to 1974, taxes and profits from Daqing given to the state was 11 times the capital that the state invested in Daqing.[129] From 1960 to 1984, the huge Daqing oilfield accounted for well over 50 percent of China's annual production during that period and turned over RMB 68.1 billion in profits and taxes to the state — roughly 20 times the value of state investment in Daqing.[130] Daqing led the nation as the single largest revenue earner for the state, no less than three percent of total revenue that the state earned from all enterprise profits and taxes.[131] Its petroleum exports also became a major source of foreign currency earnings for the PRC. Daqing was in fact one of the few sectors of growth in the Chinese economy during this period.[132]

DAQING'S MATURATION

Constant renewal was integrated into the Daqing system. According to the New China News Agency (NCNA or *Xinhua*)'s 2 January 1966 edition: "The people of Taching (Daqing) are not resting on their laurels. They know that things are in a constant state of development and change. And the increased production has certainly given rise to changes in the oil formations. They have therefore set up an extensive network of posts for studying the changes and recording them on detailed diagrams, charts, and models in the central control office in order to maintain their grasp on the whole situation".[133] According to the *Xinhua* news agency's commentary on Daqing on 7 January 1973, every oil extraction worker is responsible for overlooking several oil and water wells located far apart, gathering 62 facts under

[127] Chan, L.W. (1974), p. 11.
[128] Cheng, C. (1976), p. 59.
[129] Ibid., p. 156.
[130] Lieberthal, K. and Oksenberg, M. (1986), p. 64.
[131] Ibid., p. 65.
[132] Spence, J. (1999), p. 597.
[133] Ling, H. C. (1975), p. 151.

19 headings for each well every day, resulting in an accumulation of hundreds of thousands of facts collected on a daily basis.[134] One example is Hsin Yu-ho (Xin Yuhe) who, for many years, examined a 1,500-meter long wire cable inch by inch before using it for dewaxing.[135]

Daqing also organized its workers into "technical innovation groups" to draw people from different technical backgrounds together to provide solutions for the dynamic needs of the industry. Some of the results of these innovation groups were detailed in a *Xinhua* commentary entitled *Ta-ch'ing Oil Field* dated 29 October 1972: "Workers of the coking workshop improved the bit for clearing coke and simplified work processes. They improved the redistillation tower after more than 50 experiments and doubled its capacity by just adding four valves and 20 meters of pipes. The principle of industry and frugality is observed and local methods are used to achieve high speed and good quality. The workers used 40 old valves and 800 meters of discarded pipes to improve the dewaxing units. They also shortened the wax filtering period from three hours to 80 minutes."[136] These innovation groups were examples of systemic units formed to stimulate incremental improvements of the overall system in an effort to foster self-reliance in the industry. Self-reliance would become an important principle of Daqing.

---

[134] Ibid., p. 240.

[135] Ibid.

[136] Ling, H. C. (1975), p. 216.

Chapter

3

Daqing-ism

As Daqing's progress consolidated, longer-term planning was possible for China's policy-makers. Increasingly from 1962 on, Mao Zedong worried about the future destiny of the PRC after his death. Mao had anxieties of a fate that awaited China similar to that of the Soviet Union after the demise of Stalin. Specifically, Mao was worried that revolutionary enthusiasm and fervor might dissipate, an entrenched technocratic class and revolutionary elite would dominate the Communist Party and the quest for a communist society would be abandoned as a result. Mao visualized the bureaucratic class as a "bourgeoisie", "a class sharply opposed to the working class and the poor and lower-middle peasants".[1]

Mao embarked on a quest to re-install ideological vigor within the Party and Chinese society. He began to re-think his views of generalists and functional specialists among the top Communist leadership and eyed some of them with skepticism and suspicion, often evaluating and testing to see who were loyal to his vision, socialist orthodoxy and

[1] Dittmer, L. (1974). *Liu Shao-ch'i and the Chinese Cultural Revolution*, p. 47. Berkeley, LA and London: University of California Press.

ideological ideals. He yearned for the appearance of individuals who appeared to exhibit his values, and he sought to identify policies and organizational units which exemplified his ideas in practice. Daqing loomed large on Mao's horizon.The success of Daqing was to be used as a universal bearer of political legitimacy that could be sustained ideologically through mass propaganda to become a dominant site of national attention on Maoist construction.

The Petroleum Faction emerged as a ready-made solution to Mao's quest for ideological re-invigoration. The Daqing narrative's momentum gathered strength. Institutional expansion at Daqing was accompanied by the construction of ideological justifications for its propagation to other institutions. Mao wanted to turn Daqing into a national model and jolt the PRC's bureaucracy into activity and ideological fervor again in a bid to dispel what he perceived as the sluggishness and inflexibility of the economic specialists among the top leaders. Daqing's visible results helped convince Mao to make peace with the fact that not all specialists were counter-productive to the Revolution. In late 1964, Mao called for significant changes in the drafts of the 3rd Five-Year Plan, but his suggestions only received a partial response from the PRC elite.[2]

Disappointed, Mao summoned Yu Qiuli, Kang Shien, and others to head a new planning body to disseminate the Daqing experience for an entire range of political, industrial and bureaucratic outfits. Mao also transferred staff members from Daqing and the Petroleum Industries Ministry to his top policy-planning organs and entrenched them to help him achieve his industrial planning in China.[3] At the same time, Daqing operatives were deployed as the shock troops of Mao's publicity assault. Daqing was going to be brought closer to the people and be part of the institutions of mass culture and mass politics; its experiences would merge into public gatherings, media, radio talks and mass circulars. Mass media allowed swelling ranks of ordinary Chinese to sample the offerings of Daqing modernity. Daqing assumed central importance in official Chinese propaganda and discourse.

---

[2] Lieberthal, K. and Oksenberg, M. (1986), p. 166.

[3] Spence, J. (1999), p. 563.

In December 1963, Yu Qiuli and Kang Shien narrated the developmental experience of Daqing to a large gathering of cadres of central organs and Bejing Municipality.[4] This meeting initiated and catalyzed the process of Daqing becoming a national model and its leading developers becoming the stewards to navigate the entire Chinese economy. The December 1963 meeting gave Daqing widespread publicity with Mao's blessings. In late 1963, Mao promulgated that, in industry, China should "learn from Daqing".[5] Such publicity of the oilfield's developmental experience had the intended effect of establishing a universal language to be used by industrial technocrats and planners, as Daqing-ism tried to provide a unified basis for all industrial developments in China.

Mao's endorsement helped industrial technocracy blend in easily with ideological development. Technical personnel, once considered outside the Communist circle of trust, too bourgeoisie and reeked of pre-1949 China, were now basking in the ideological limelight. The PRC's Daqing engineering corps was entrusted with the task of "gaining glory for the nation, gaining honor for the people (*weiguozhengguang, weiminzhengqi*)" through their "heroic spirit and a strong sense of responsibility (*yingxiongqigai he qianglie de zherengan*)".[6]

Yu and Kang informed the audience that Daqing then had proven reserves of over 2.67 billion tons, and was churning out oil at the rate of 6 million tons per year.[7] As a triumphant note, it was declared that state investment of 7.01 billion yuan had already been recovered, and Daqing had already generated 3.05 billion yuan in state revenue.[8] Outside tangible progress, Yu and Kang claimed that Daqing had also trained its personnel and equipped them with technological proficiency, organizational/management skills, discipline and courage to overcome environmental hardship. Students mobilized

---

[4] Lieberthal, K. and Oksenberg, M. (1986), p. 167.

[5] Spence, J. (1999), p. 563.

[6] Zhongguo Lianyou Gongye (China Oil-Refining Industry), Editorial Team (1989), p. 77.

[7] Lieberthal, K. and Oksenberg, M. (1986), p. 167.

[8] Ibid.

to work in Daqing were on half-study, half-work systems which enabled them to be paid and educated at the same time while full-time employment was enhanced with annual payments in work points calculated from the revenue of all the unit-responsibilities which the employees operated.[9]

A successful industrial example was valued by centralized planning as an existing model that acted as an economical standard teaching tool for emulation to speed up the learning process. On 26 Dec 1963, Mao promulgated the slogan "Industry Study Daqing."[10] Whether as architects of Daqing's production or participants in China's industrial modernity, Daqing's technocratic class stood at the vanguard of the effort to construct China's oil self-reliance. The use of technocrats as examples represented an innovation in state techniques for mobilization.

Moreover, such publicity was able to stimulate competition amongst units engaged in the same industry to out-compete each other to receive state praise and hit state quota targets, acting as a form of pressure on non-performing units.[11] With Daqing as a standard, units unable to match Daqing's accomplishments were admonished publicly through the *Renmin Ribao* (*People's Daily*), for example Maoming Petroleum Company was chastised for not matching up to Daqing's achievements and for not conscientiously implementing "Chairman Mao's revolutionary line".[12]

Although even Daqing's own planners may not have been sufficiently persuaded by the logic of Daqing's applicability to a multitude of industries and organizations, to the ideologues, Daqing's relevance to China was unimpeachable. Some planners might have silently questioned the wisdom of dogmatically applying the Daqing model to all industries but none spoke out in an era which was unforgiving on non-conformity. Optimism in the applicability of Daqing-ism to industries was in part a consequence of the underlying ideological views of its proponents.

[9] Chan, L. W. (1974), p. 10.

[10] Lieberthal, K. and Oksenberg, M. (1986), p. 167.

[11] Chan, L. W. (1974), p. 6.

[12] Ibid.

On 5 February 1964, the Party Central Committee set out to put down Daqing's lesson in writing for all its cadre members. They disseminated a classified circular to lower level committees, pointing out that Daqing was a model of "more, faster, better and more economical" development.[13] The same circular informed the Communist hierarchy that Daqing had systematically studied and applied the experience of political work in the PLA while closely integrating political thought, revolutionary fervor/ardor, and scientific management. Its experience was applicable and adaptable to all units (*danwei*) down the Communist hierarchy to the mass organizations.

After this circular was issued, a movement to study Daqing gathered strength and became a full-fledged national campaign with Mao's inspiration and encouragement. Daqing was no longer the sole property of the oil industry technocracy. It was promoted with equal fervor by participants inside and outside of the oil technocracy in the hope of conjuring up new relationships between state, society and industry. In proportion to Daqing's material importance, a sizable ideological assault was prepared for the masses.

The mass consumption of Daqing-ism began with the article *Daqing Jingshen, Daqing Ren* (Daqing Spirit, Daqing Man) published in the *People's Daily* on 20 April 1964 when the oilfield was revealed to the public at large for the first time. The article touted Daqing's relevance to China's path to oil self-reliance (*shiyou zigei*).[14] It also coined the phrase "*Daqing Jingshen*" (Daqing spirit) to signify the close relationship between political breakthrough and scientific attitude.[15] The massive mass media assault was then extended to other major dailies and more copies of *People's Daily*, including the *Worker's Daily* (*Gongren Ribao*) on 1 January and 1 March 1966, *People's Daily* (*Renmin Ribao*) on 1 October 1964 and 1 September 1966, with the same exhortations of learning from Daqing.[16]

---

[13] Lieberthal, K. and Oksenberg, M. (1986), p. 167.

[14] Gaimusho Keizaikyoku Keizaitogoka (Japan's Ministry of Foreign Affairs Economics Bureau Economics Statistics Section) (1970), p. 168.

[15] Ibid., p. 168–169.

[16] Ibid.

In January 1966, the *People's Daily* started a new column specially focused on "learning from" and "catching up with" Daqing.[17]

Daqing was also being reshaped as Mao's icon of socialist orthodoxy. Meanwhile, at the same time, Mao was busy identifying organizations and people who matched his core values and was handpicking his "revolutionary successors". Daqing was one of the standards used in this aspect as reflected in his speeches from this time throughout 1964.[18] Public campaigns before the advent of technological mass media like radio and television became the preferred medium through which the achievements and influence of Daqing first penetrated the communities and imbued Chinese society with oil fever.

Speaking at the Spring Festival on 13 February eight days after the party circular on Daqing, Mao noted that in order to remedy certain deficiencies in industrial work, organizations "must study the PLA and study Daqing of the Ministry of Petroleum."[19] After mentioning the relatively low investment in Daqing and noting it produced considerable oil after three years of development, Mao succinctly praised the oil-field: "The investment was little, the time was short and the effectiveness was high."[20] He repeated himself: "Every ministry ought to study the ministry of petroleum, study the PLA and grasp good experience."[21] The ideologically-potent Daqing was placed at the heart of Chinese modernity.

While Daqing was geographically and physically far from urban Chinese centers of power and economy, its depiction in the mass media drew on a new sense of connectedness between all potential beneficiaries of its developmental experience and the remotely-located oilfield. Daqing-ism had grown at the national, industrial and societal levels, all necessary to make the movement a comprehensive success. Daqing represented the idea that once the power of ideology was released, its potential for progress and transformation was enormous.

---

[17] Ling, H. C. (1975), p. 131.

[18] Lieberthal, K. and Oksenberg, M. (1986), p. 168.

[19] Ibid.

[20] Ibid.

[21] Ibid.

One of the most comprehensive and scathing media assault on foreign assertions that China was poor in oil came from the article published by New China News Agency (NCNA) on 2 December 1971 entitled *Ministry Article Refutes Theory "China is Poor in Oil"* (Peking Domestic Service in Mandarin 1030 GMT 2 Dec 71B). It attacked almost every non-PRC figure in the Chinese oil industry. Directed at the Americans, the article charged: "Since the beginning of the 20th century, a number of so-called U.S. 'scholars' and 'authorities', proceeding from an idealist point of view, came to China, vigorously spreading the fallacy that "China is poor in oil." They babbled: "There is little chance of finding oil in southeastern China, there is still less chance of finding it in southwestern China, a small amount of petroleum is being produced in northwestern China, but it looks like there will not be any major oilfield, like northern China, there is no large amount of petroleum in northeastern China." The article concluded that according to the Americans, "it is impossible for China to produce large amounts of petroleum."[22]

The NCNA article then proceeded to attack the pre-war and wartime Nationalist allies of the Americans: "A number of bourgeois 'experts' and 'authorities' of old China who clung to U.S. imperialism also clamored that 'China is vast but lacks raw materials. Oil deposits in China are low.' It was under the influence of these reactionary theories that only a few small oilfields were put into operation throughout the nation in the 45 years from 1904 to 1948, producing only some few hundred thousand tons of petroleum, and that the Chinese people had to use 'foreign oil'."[23]

According to this NCNA article, the PRC government was able to circumvent these misleading thoughts through scientific application of rationality and developing their own ideas and theories in prospecting for oil. The article claimed: "Once, in the course of surveying and drilling in an area, they (Daqing workers) came across a red stratum. According to the idea that 'there is no oil in the red stratum,' there would have been no need to continue the survey and drilling

---

[22] Ling, H. C. (1975), p. 188.

[23] Ibid.

work. After summing up their experience in practice, however, the workers and technicians came to understand that, although the red stratum could not produce oil by itself, there is still the possibility of a big oilfield if good conditions for oil exist and if there are good oil-bearing strata in nearby areas. With this understanding, they made a detailed analysis of the actual geological conditions and continued to survey and drill in greater depth."[24] The commentary asserted that the Daqing workers were now self-reliant in ideas and technical theories about oil prospecting and management.

The commentary also claimed that China developed these ideas through trial and error: "In the past when prospecting for oil in some areas, the masses found that the calcareous rock stratum was thin and thought that there was little or no possibility of finding oil and that they could not accomplish anything there. They only tried to find oil in sandstone areas. The result was that they prospected for 20 years with their efforts concentrated on the sandstone areas and ignored a vast expanse of land which they should have surveyed. Through practice by the broad masses of workers and technicians, it was proven by much data that a thin calcareous rock stratum can also provide good conditions for oil. The masses drilled high-yield oil wells in such areas, thus emancipating large areas of calcareous rock stratum from the stereotype of being poor in oil."[25]

The commentary then asserted the rational superiority of science in reversing these highlighted early examples of foreign opinion of China's oil potential: "A correct conclusion can be drawn only through a large amount of practical work and a comprehensive analysis of all data obtained in prospecting. Any simple assertion or denial will lead to an erroneous metaphysical conclusion."[26]

Other than the mass media, representative of contemporary popular depictions of Daqing is the book *Zhongguo Shiyou Dahui Zhan* (*A Chinese Great Battle for Oil*) by Chen DaoKuo published in 1994. The writer stated that the book could be read as "history or literature

[24] Ibid., pp. 191–192.
[25] Ibid., p. 192.
[26] Ibid.

or even social sciences".[27] Chen was intimately connected to the Chinese oil industry and had conducted interviews at Daqing and met its pioneers. At the same time, he wrote in eloquent prose characterised by literary construction. Herein lay the reason for his book's popular appeal as it was touted to be a must-read, failure in doing so would result in regret (*chishu bugebudu, budu biding gandao yihan*)'.[28]

Some of the timeless themes included the historically exceptionalized image of China's oil poverty and how this humiliating "hat" was removed with Daqing's "great battle for oil (*shiyou dahuizhan*)". The first page of the book starts with the imperialist taunt of an American military analyst published in the 1961 issue of an oil periodical (*Shijie Shiyou*) who considered the obstacles towards the PRC achieving "self-reliance status (*zigeijizhu*)" to be insurmountable, including China's "teapot-sized refinery (*xiaochahushi de lianyou zhuangzhi*)".[29] This prediction was squashed in "a peculiar moment (*qitede shikong zhijian*)" by China's Daqing achievements, so begins the story.[30] The clean break from the past suggests somewhat deterministically that China would be able to pick itself up, starting with having found its own oil as the lifeblood of modern industry after suffering centuries of humiliation under imperialistic powers and becoming self-reliant in the context of self-isolation.

ACTS OF HEROISM

Human achievements at Daqing should not be under-rated. Oil personnel had to work in a harsh natural environment during bitter cold months in January and February (sometimes at –30 degrees Celsius)[31] and scant material comfort. Modern equipment was inadequate with few motorized vehicles and accessible roads. The workers overcame

[27] Chen, D. K. (1994), cover.

[28] Ibid.

[29] Ibid., p. 1.

[30] Ibid., p. 2.

[31] Bartke, W. (1977), pp. 75 and 77.

technological deficiencies through sheer self-reliant brute labor. There were also no habitable houses and the workers had to pitch tents for their accommodation.[32] In Leslie Chan's account, some workers even had to put up in stables and holes in the ground.[33] There was one instance when telephone wires for communication were damaged by a storm and two workers, Mao Xiaozhong (Mao Hsiao-chung) and Xiao Chuanfa (Hsiao Chuan-Fa), rejoined the wire that snapped by holding them together so that phone calls could get through.[34] They were led by the then First Party Secretary at Daqing, 45-year old Long March veteran Yu Qiuli, who doubled up as the Minister of Petroleum during the first year of Daqing and directed operations with only one arm.[35]

Backbreaking labor was also involved as workers used shoulder poles to lug the heavy rigs to their sites and, when there was no running water for drilling, they ferried the water to the site basin by basin from a small lake one mile away.[36] Before spur lines were built, Daqing riggers dragged their equipment with ropes, tipping them with crowbars and easing them along wooden logs[37] because of the lack of cranes and tractors.[38] Sixty-ton drillers were transported inch by inch, yard by yard, to the site in this manner usually lasting a total of three days and nights.[39] Due to the waxy nature of Daqing crude, heaters had to be installed along the pipes to prevent the oil from coagulating at 28 degrees Celsius. However, lighting the heater itself became a risky business because workers often had their faces blackened by strong gusts of wind or their hair or eyebrows singed.[40] Daqing workers' hardship gradually evolved into an ideological slogan known as the "Daqing spirit" which incorporated

---

[32] Lieberthal, K. and Oksenberg, M. (1986), p. 160.

[33] Chan, L. W. (1974), p. 9.

[34] Ling, H. C. (1975), p. 240.

[35] Lieberthal, K. and Oksenberg, M. (1986), p. 157.

[36] Ibid., p. 160.

[37] Ibid.

[38] Foreign Languages Press (1977), p. 7.

[39] Lieberthal, K. and Oksenberg, M. (1986), p. 160.

[40] Chen, D. K. (1994), p. 290.

features like "hauling and carrying the machines manually", "starting a revolution with five shovels", etc and other incredible human feats against Nature.[41]

One exemplary worker to emerge during this period whose name would become associated with the Chinese oil industry itself is Ironman Wang Chin-hsi (Wang Jinxi, 1923–1970).[42] In the Cultural Revolution-era publication *Daqingren de Gushi* (*Story of the People at Daqing*) written by the *Daqing Youtian Gongren Xiezhuozu* (The Writers' Team for Daqing) published in 1971, Ironman Wang was depicted as a Daqing pioneer with fiery passion for self-reliance. On the eve of the discovery of Daqing and on his way to Beijing to attend a national conference, Wang apparently saw a vehicle with a contraption strapped to its back and asked what its function was.

When he was informed that the device was a natural gas tank to power the vehicle, he was said to be filled with rage and could not accept the fact that China did not have adequate oil supplies to power their own vehicles. Filled with anxiety, Wang wondered to himself: "As workers in the Chinese oil industry, how could they let China go through such a crisis and allow imperialism mock the Chinese people? (*zhuowei yige zhongguode shiyou gongren, nengran guojia zhuo zheme dadenan, nengran diguozhuyikan womende xiaohua ma?*)".[43]

Wang was also indignant at the fact that foreign oil often carried a host of difficult and oppressive conditions including oil products that were not needed by China, prices were allegedly higher than equivalent volume sold to other countries and, even more outrageous, soil, water, horse manure and high-heeled shoes were found in the imported aviation oil.[44] Nationalism and the desire for self-reliance were now articulated, verbalized and contextualized.

---

[41] Foreign Languages Press, (1977), p. 7.

[42] Wang, Y. (1992), p. 81. *Zhongguo Shiyou Shihua (About the History of China's Oil Industry)*, China: Shiyou Gongye Chubanshe.

[43] Daqing Youtian Gongren Xiezhuozu (The Writers' Team for Daqing) (1971). *Daqingren de Gushi* (*Story of the People at Daqing*), p. 3. Shanghai: Shanghai Renmin Chubanshe (Shanghai People's Publishing House).

[44] Ibid., p. 4.

According to Part Five of a New China News Agency (NCNA) commentary dated 2 January 1973 and entitled *Ta-Ch'ing Oilfield*, Wang alighted from the train and immediately led his No. 1205 drilling team to Daqing without taking a rest.[45] Wang slept on a pile of drill pipes with a drill bit as his pillow.[46] Wang was hospitalized while putting up the derrick and, on the midnight of the day of the injury, he secretly went back to the work site and directed his team while leaning on crutches.[47]

Then he did the unthinkable: "During the drilling operation, there was imminent danger of a blowout which could have buried the derrick. The usual method of preventing it was to pour in heavy spar, but that would have taken too long to bring to the site. Making a quick decision, Wang Chin-hsi [Ironman Wang or Wang Jinxi] ordered that eight bags of cement that were at hand be poured into a mortar pit. They had no mixer, so Ironman Wang jumped into the pit, followed by two other members of the team. The men worked like Trojans in mixing the mortar, and prevented a blowout. When he was helped out of the pit, Ironman Wang could not stand. His legs were bruised and aching and his hands were blistered."[48]

Relying on manpower when mechanized equipment was absent was a form of battle of wills that the Communist Party used to demonstrate the doctrine of self-reliance. Unable to import equipment, given both US and Soviet hostilities in its international relations, China had to rely on its own manpower to make up for the lack of equipment. As depicted in Chinese oil literature printed during the Cultural Revolution, Ironman Wang's solutions and responses to areas of foreign dependence or simply lack of equipment were to substitute them with manpower. For example, when there was a deficiency in water or equipment to ferry water for the drilling process, Ironman Wang ordered his fellow workers to scoop water

[45] Ling, H. C. (1975), p. 238.

[46] Ibid.

[47] Ibid.

[48] Ling, H. C. (1975), pp. 238–239.

with a facewash basin barrel by barrel, basin by basin from a hole in a frozen body of water and pour them into the drill spot.[49]

There were other stories of heroic acts. According to the same NCNA commentary dated 2 January 1973 entitled *Ta-Ch'ing Oilfield*, the leader of Daqing's first extraction team and Communist party member Hsueh Kuo-pang (Xue Guobang) sank makeshift oil storage pits into the frozen earth because pipelines and metal tanks were not available at the time and, holding a steam hose in his hand, he waded waist-deep in the freezing oil to melt it.[50] The fluid was pumped into railway tank cars to be taken out.[51] The publication *Bainian Shiyou (100 Years of Petroleum) 1878-2000* published by China's Dangdai Zhongguo Chubanshe in 2002 described Xue's heroic act in the following passage:

> "Xue Guobang was a team leader from Yumen oilfield who led 20 oilfield workers to settle down at this wild land [Daqing]. Armed with self-made wooden winches, he was in charge of over 100 square meters of oilfield. To ensure that the first batch of oil shipment targeted on 1 June 1960 (Liuyi) was shipped out successfully, he used his hands to pull together a burning steam pipe and jumped into the oil pool to melt the coagulated oil. Although his hands were badly burnt, he insisted on completing the job."[52]

In another story within the same commentary, engineering team leader Chu Hung-chang (Zhu Hongzhang) found a leak in the pipeline and wrapped his hand in a towel and helped the welder to fix it because no gloves were at hand; the sparks from the welding narrowly missed burning his hand".[53] Such feats of human endurance demonstrated at Daqing could not entirely be accounted for by physical endurance alone. There was also a strong sense of camaraderie and egalitarianism as all Daqing personnel, regardless of rank, from leading cadres and experts to technicians and ordinary workers,

[49] Daqing Youtian Gongren Xiezhuozu (The Writers' Team for Daqing) (1971), p. 15.

[50] Ling, H. C. (1975), p. 239.

[51] Ibid.

[52] Wen, *et al.* (2002), pp. 113-114.

[53] Ling, H. C. (1975), p. 239.

contributed to the construction of mud houses for their combating the first winter.[54] The slogan then for this unmitigated unity as described in PRC oil literature was "*quanguo yipanqi* (the entire state is one single chessboard)".[55]

All people from the center and periphery of power in PRC could learn from such examples. Daqing's workers called each other "brothers (*xiongdi*)", underlining the familial atmosphere.[56] Other slogans included "*sannian gongxia* Songliao (Let's take down Songliao in three years)" and "*jinkuai zai dongfang zaodao dayoutian* (Quickly located a large oilfield in China's East)".[57] Incorporated into a rhetoric of brotherhood was a feeling of togetherness in a grand project that drove Daqing workers on to achieve record-breaking feats, including drilling more than 90 wells in 1961, a total of 32,746 m in depth.[58]

On 29 September 1966, the New China News Agency (NCNA or *Xinhua*) reported that the top Chinese leadership received and hosted representatives from the five outstanding units in the Chinese oil industry including the Nos. 1202 and 1205 drilling teams at the Daqing oilfield.[59] They gathered in Beijing on 27 September 1966 and made reports to more than 2000 representatives from various departments of the central authorities in charge of capital construction where the outstanding drillers shared their experiences.[60] The family and dependents of the top drillers also shared the spotlight as being successful laborers.[61] Even Gu Mu, chairperson of the State Capital

---

[54] Lieberthal, K. and Oksenberg, M. (1986), p. 160.

[55] Zhang, W. (1999). Zhongguo Shiyou Kantan Zhanlue Dongyi de Zhongda Tupo (The Great Breakthrough Behind Chinese Oil Exploration's Shift Eastwards). In *Dangdai Zhongguo Youqi Kantan Zhongda Faxian (The Important Discoveries of Contemporary China's Oil and Gas Exploration)* Zhang, W. (ed.) p. 263. Beijing: Shiyou Gongye Chubanshe.

[56] Beijing Chubanshe (1966). *Xiang Daqingshi Qiye Xuexi (Learn from Daqing-style Industries)*, p. 62. Beijing: Beijingchubanshe.

[57] Zhang, W. (1999), p. 263.

[58] Ling, H. C. (1975), p. 127.

[59] Ibid., p. 154.

[60] Ibid., pp. 155–156.

[61] Ling, H. C. (1975), p. 154.

Construction Commission extended his congratulations and paid respect to the drillers and other oilfield heroes "on behalf of the several million workers in the capital construction field".[62]

Bartke indicated that two drilling teams set national records in 1966 with each of them exceeding the 60,000 m depth mark in seven months and 21 days, beating the previous record of 40,816 m held by the Soviet IB Poljakovski drilling team in 1965.[63] Bartke added that the Chinese carried out their daily drilling with a single drill bit 1,000 m in length. According to PRC declarations, the 1,205 drilling team went on to break their own record by drilling a total length of 100,000 m in depth in 1966.[64] They were also able to drill high-quality wells in a mere 27 hours and 40 minutes and carried out oil exploration over a distance of 21.8 km per day.[65] In the 10 years between 1960 and 1969, the 1,205 team apparently drilled a total of 376,980 m and set a new world record of 127,000 m in 1971.[66]

The Western press was much more guarded and cautious in acknowledging such feats. An icon from these record-breaking feats was Ironman Wang Jingxi. For example, *Newsweek* on 27 October 1975 described him thus: "Wang Chin-shi is known as the 'Ironman,' a determined, fearless foreman who in 1960 as head of the legendary drill team 1,205 brought in the first big gusher at what is now the mammoth Taching oil field ... if even half of his storied oil-field exploits actually took place, his status is well-deserved."[67] PRC's efforts in releasing news of world record-breaking to the world at large but especially to Chinese society allowed everybody to share the sense of pride and identify with the sacrifice and the selfless martyrdom of Daqing individuals. Efforts to mobilize a community of

---

[62] Ibid., p. 156.

[63] Bartke, W. (1977), p. 72.

[64] Ling, H. C. (1975), p. 164.

[65] Ibid.

[66] Bartke, W. (1977), p. 72.

[67] Bernardo, R. M. (1977). *Popular Management and Pay in China*, p. 177. Quezon City, Philippines: University of the Philippines Press.

support and recognition for the record breakers led to the formation of new linkages between state, society and industry.

THE MODEL OILFIELD

Daqing's pristine facilities did not escape the pervasive ideological gaze either. The reason why there was not a single case of lung disease, according to the publication *Zoudaqingde Daolu Bandaqingshi Qiye* (*Walk the Path of Daqing and Carry Out Daqing-style Industries*) by the Guangdong People's Publishing Bureau, was partly the result of following Daqing's strict adherence to the principle of "ever-strengthening the management of industries (*buduan jiaqiang qiye guanli*)", a slogan related to the "four stricts (*siyan*)".[68]

Here, ideology was mixed with the scientific tinge of welfarism by combining Mao's entrenched ideological maxims with production theories of "ever-improving safety and air circulation (*gaishan anquan he tongfeng tiaojian*)" through air filtration (*jinghua kongqi*).[69] The constant monitoring of untouched corners of production lapses such as air circulation in this case is a Taylorist impulse to continually rationalize production processes to maximize output. This lethal combination of scientific and ideological rationality was cited as the main reason for the non-existence of lung disease at Daqing.

Apparently, Daqing's example also highlighted the effectiveness of mixing technical experts with workers and so this was further rationalized and institutionalized in the revival of Daqing-ism through the formation of layman-technical expert teams who pooled their resources to upgrade productive skills and to design new products.[70] To a certain extent, this seemed to work, as a University of Philippines

---

[68] Guangdongshen Geming Weiyuanhui Gongshe Bangongshi/Zhengzhibu (The Guangdong Revolutionary Committee Administration and Political Affairs Bureaus) (1973). *Zoudaqingde Daolu Bandaqingshi Qiye* (*Walk the Path of Daqing and Carry Out Daqing-style Industries*), p. 21. China: Guangdong Renmin Chubanshe.

[69] Ibid., p. 21.

[70] Ibid., p. 113.

professor, Robert Bernardo, who studied management in China cited the example of a pipeline construction from Daqing to Beijing where "the engineering and designing personnel joined efforts with the workers to make surveys along the line and work out several draft designs on the route for the pipeline and the location of booster stations."[71] He continued: "After making repeated comparisons and soliciting suggestions from all quarters, they finally decided on an economical and rational route which saved the state a considerable amount of investments."[72] Bernardo noted the informal and intuitive nature of such interactions.

Similarly within the ideological realm, Daqing's middle school was named as the Ironman School as it supposedly distilled the teachings of Wang Jingxi and mass-produced them for the workers at Daqing. Set up in May 1961 by Wang himself, the school started with six students and grew to over 1,300 in 1977 with 75 teaching staff members in charge of a nine-year curriculum.[73] The Ironman himself was said to have declared that, since Mao had placed such a premium on educating and bringing up the offspring of Daqing staff members, the school had to be set up no matter how difficult the task was.[74] The school started off from humble beginnings as a five square meter dug-out pit covered with a torn piece of canvas and later included a toilet specially for the kids' safety.[75]

The Ironman's selflessness was also highlighted when he donated his own well-used radio set and work desk to the school. When someone commented that the school resembled a chicken's cage more than it did a school, Ironman burst into fury and countered by saying

---

[71] Bernardo, R. M. (1977), p. 162.

[72] Ibid., p. 163.

[73] Daqing Youtian Tieren Xuexiao Dangzhibu (Daqing Oilfield Ironman School Party Branch) (1977). Yong Daqing Jingshen ban Xuexiao Peiyang Tierenshi de Jiebanren (Using the Daqing Spirit to Manage a School to Produce Ironman-like Successors). In *Gongye Zhanxian de Xianyan Hongqi* (*The Brightly-Colored Red Flag of the Industrial Battlefront*), p. 279. China: Renminchubanshe.

[74] Ibid., p. 280.

[75] Ibid., pp. 280 and 281.

that the school was set up for revolutionary purposes and not capitalistic ideals.[76] The purpose of education was not to create "Western-style scholars" but to produced proletariat revolutionary successors.[77] The Ironman himself had proletariat roots, starting off as a cattle herder at the age of six,[78] a beggar together with his blind father at the age of 8[79] and, at the age of 15, became a worker at an oilfield, finally embarking on what would become his lifelong career.[80]

Ironman became its first principal and hired a fulltime teacher. In the first lesson that he taught, Ironman reminded the students that Mao played a major role in their educational opportunities and urged them not to forget this deed and to follow Mao in his revolutionary ideals. At the end of 1965, Ironman persuaded some reluctant veteran workers to join the teaching staff at the school, overcoming their fears of not being qualified to be teaching instructors.[81]

WAR MOBILIZATION

The military importance of Daqing was also dramatized with analogies to the same spirit needed to "drive out Japanese imperialism".[82] In fact, Daqing was sometimes referred to as a 'battle zone (*zhanqu*)'.[83] In the days leading up to the discovery of Daqing, the historical biography of Daqing *Zhongguo Shiyou Dahui Zhan* (*A Chinese Great Battle for Oil*) published by the People's Liberation Army press Bayi Chubanshe quoted Yu Qiuli as saying: "Songliao is a piece of fat meat, we want to first eat the fat meat!

---

[76] Ibid., p. 281.

[77] Ibid., p. 291.

[78] Chen, D. K. (1994), p. 153.

[79] Ling, H. C. (1975), p. 238.

[80] Chen, D. K. (1994), p. 153.

[81] Daqing Youtian Tieren Xuexiao Dangzhibu (Daqing Oilfield Ironman School Party Branch) (1977), p. 283.

[82] Foreign Languages Press (1977), p. 9.

[83] Chen, D. K. (1994), p. 268.

You guys (signaling to his colleagues/subordinates), quick go, quick! This is war! Time is about military and time is victory (*Songliao shi yikuai feirou, women yaoxianchi feirou! Nimen yao gankuai shangqu, kuai! Zheshi dazhangle! Shijian jiushi jundui, shijian juishi shengli le!*)".[84]

On the eve of the Daqing discovery, under pressure from Chairman Mao who asked Yu Qiuli for some "good news (*ni nail youmeiyou yidian haoxiaoxi*)", Yu Qiuli told the Chairman that Songliao had made progress.[85] Unknown to him, Premier Zhou Enlai had already reported Songliao's oil potential to the Chairman in preparation for what Mao styled as '*Shiyou Dahuizhan* (*A Chinese Great Battle for Oil*)'.[86] The phrase '*Dahuizhan*' had also been used to mean guerilla warfare during the anti-Japanese resistance period. Associating the prospecting of what would become Daqing oilfield in Songliao with the Sino-Japanese war enabled Zhou to secure Mao's approval in allocating the same intensity of resources to the oil industry.

Yu Qiuli's experience with mobilization of troops to fight the Japanese was considered useful for this purpose and the Chinese leadership was hoping to tap into Yu's experience in gathering sizable forces at a short time or making do with less than adequate manpower for difficult tasks. They had precedents to bank on. Even though there was a shortage of available able-bodied young men to fight the enemy during WWII, Yu was known for his legendary ability to mobilize and train a force of 300 "ruffians and mountain bandits (*xiaoju shanlin bingfei*)" to resist three enemy brigades of over 5,000 men for two to three months at the frontlines.[87] Yu hoped to tap the People's Liberation Army for the same purpose, shaping untrained soldiers and 30,000 demobilized soldiers to prospect for oil in the Songliao plains.[88]

---

[84] Ibid., pp. 41–42.

[85] Ibid., p. 117.

[86] Ibid., p. 118.

[87] Ibid., p. 120.

[88] Ibid., pp. 120–121, 123.

In addition, Yu replicated his battlefield strategies for Daqing's exploratory organization. During wartime, he had a habit of setting up command posts near the frontlines where shots could be heard and close enough to observe the actual war situation.[89] For Songliao, he established the headquarters of the organization near the site of exploratory works[90] so that he could similarly see and observe day-to-day operations at the worksites. To the Chinese imagination detailed in the Daqing biographical publication *Zhongguo Shiyou Dahui Zhan* (*A Chinese Great Battle for Oil*) published by the military press Bayi Chubanshe in 1994, it was not simply oil prospecting but "the start of an important smokeless great battle (*yige meiyou xiaoyan paohuode zhongdazhan yijijiang kaishile*)".[91]

In popular historical fiction depicting Daqing's oil struggles, Yu Qiuli the pioneer behind the oilfield was apparently fond of letting out a battle cry during the excavation process. This was said to have originated from the anti-Japanese war when Yu trained his troops to let out a cry "with the might of lions and tigers (*shizi laohu de weifeng*)" when charging forward. Part of the reason for doing this was to counter the "jarring cries and shouts (*dahan dajiao*)" of Japanese troops in battle.[92]

By implication, it would also mean that fighting the environmental odds of Daqing exploitation could be equated to fighting the Japanese themselves. Having joined the Red Amy in 1929 at the age of 14,[93] Yu Qiuli used the 8th Route Army — of which he was a member — and their battles with Japanese troops as analogies to dramatize the difficulties of oil exploitation. He tapped the collective memory of fighting the war to convince younger generations of oil workers and technicians about the need for dogged perseverance to reach for success in the face of a determined enemy.[94]

---

[89] Ibid., p. 125.

[90] Ibid.

[91] Ibid., p. 123.

[92] Ibid., p. 52.

[93] Ibid., p. 19.

[94] Ibid., p. 215.

In the post-WWII era, readiness for war, particularly against the two "hegemonic" powers of the Soviet Union and the US, became an overt priority for developing Daqing.[95] The Chinese were convinced that, since the Sino-Soviet split, the USSR was trying to use oil blockade as a weapon against her.[96] The Vice-Chairman of the Chinese Communist Party Central Committee, Ye Jianying, stressed at the Learn from Daqing Conference that industrialization was fundamental to adequate modernization in warfare and military weapons.[97] He also stressed the importance of preventive warfare, to strengthen one's domestic defense in preparation for war.[98] Given this line of thinking, the PRC was not going to be caught again unprepared for warfare like it did in WWII.

Besides preventive warfare, military doctrines like "*jizhong youshi binli dajianmiezhan* (concentrating the elite troops for a battle of enemy elimination)"[99] were also adapted by oil institutions and departments like the *Shiyou Kexue Yanjiuyuan* (Petroleum Sciences Research Institute) to conduct their experiments and come up with optimum designs. The second Learn from Daqing national conference conjured up the Armageddon-like scenario in which the Soviet Union and US were "frenziedly expanding armaments and stepping up war preparations and a world war is bound to break out some day."[100] Military analogies reinforced and helped to highlight the adversarial dynamics in China's relations with external powers keen on limiting China's capabilities through cutting off Chinese oil availability.

---

[95] Foreign Languages Press (1977), p. 15.

[96] Cheng, C. (1976), p. 11.

[97] Renmin Chubanshe (1977). *Zhongguo Gongchangdang Zhongyang Weiyuanhui Fuzhuxi Ye Jianying Tongzhi Xai Quanguo Gongye Xuedaqinghuishang De Jianghua (The Speech Given by Vice Chairman Comrade Ye Jianying at the National Chinese Communist Party Central Committee Learn from Daqing Conference)*, p. 7. Beijing: Renmin Chubanshe.

[98] Ibid.

[99] Zhongguo Lianyou Gongye (China Oil-Refining Industry) Editorial Team (1989), p. 90.

[100] Foreign Languages Press (1977), p. 34.

Many leaders of Daqing and the oil industry in general were battle-weary hardened veterans who brought along their wartime experience to Chinese oil development. The don of the industry, Yu Qiuli, for example had fought in conflicts for most of his life. Right from the beginning when he was first inducted into the Red Army, Yu had to escape Guomindang assassins and was on the run with his two younger brothers while his mother was captured by the enemy and severely tortured.[101] Yu was appointed Minister of Petroleum Industry in February 1958.[102] Yu's warrior ethics, forged in warfare, was highlighted by the fact that, during the most crucial phases of Daqing's development, he chose to stay behind and man the oilfield instead of visiting his gravely-ill mother.[103] Yu's official memoir published by the PLA in 1996 has pictures of him dated August 1961 having lunch in Spartan settings with ground level workers.[104]

The military value of the Chinese oil industry was retained as a major feature even after Mao's death. Mao's successor Chairman Hua Guofeng declared this at The National Conference on Learning from Taching (Daqing) in Industry on 20 April 1977 at Daqing attended by 7,000 delegates representing China's major industries. He reminded those present that: "We must definitely **be ready for war** (bold-faced in original official transcripts of the speech). We cannot afford to let time slip through our fingers, as it waits for no one. Every Communist, every revolutionary and every patriot should be clear about the situation, seize the present opportune moment, strive to work well and make our country strong and prosperous as soon as possible".[105]

FOREIGN OPINIONS

There are also foreign accounts of unvoiced Chinese dissent against Daqing-ism recorded by foreign observers. For example, Judith Shapiro

---

[101] Chen, D. K. (1994), pp. 315–316.

[102] Yu, Q. (1996). *Yu Qiuli Huiyilu (Memoirs of Yu Qiuli)*. Beijing: Jiefangjun Chubanshe The PLA Press.

[103] Chen, D. K. (1994), p. 316.

[104] Yu, Q. (1996).

[105] Foreign Languages Press (1977), p. 15.

cited a retired professor of plant nutrition in recounting the pressures she felt during the Learn from Daqing era when Chinese industries and agriculture were urged to join the mad rush to achieve high production targets. To do this, they had to overcome environmental odds and barriers, just like how Daqing pioneers battled harsh conditions dished out by nature to open up Daqing. According to the retired professor, Daqing-ism at the time of conception enunciated: "When the oil workers shout with all their might, the great earth will shake and tremble". The unnamed retired professor felt that it was a mistake on the part of the planners to insist that nature be subdued as it "violates the laws of nature".[106]

Lieberthal had a theory that took the plausible middle line to explain the spectacular rise of Daqing within a short period of time, apart from designating it as purely propaganda. He attributed the accomplishments to the presence of trained technicians rather than ideological victory over nature or mind over matter. He presented the following explanation: "Our analysis of Daqing's early years does suggest two important ways in which later myths about its development were not totally accurate. First, technicians played a crucial part in the survey, exploration, and development. Amateurs did not bring a field of this magnitude into production. However, in the propaganda about Daqing, the role of technicians was understated. Technological innovation did receive emphasis, to be sure, but it frequently was attributed to the "masses" or to workers. The model heroes were the well drillers, especially Iron Man Wang Jinxi and the 1205 drilling team. One searches in vain for model technicians and laboratory teams."[107]

[106] Shapiro, J. (2001). *Mao's War Against Nature*, p. 77. New York: Cambridge University Press.

[107] Lieberthal, K. and Oksenberg, M. (1986), p. 163.

Chapter

4

The Doctrine of Self-Reliance

Daqing's early achievements from the 1960s onwards did not escape the attention of foreign observers. Vaclav Smil, well-known for his strongly-worded writings on China, attributed China's oil achievements in Daqing to the issue of probability. He argued: "China's sedimentary basins are simply too numerous and too extensive for this not to happen".[1] At the same time, despite the provenance of probability, Smil did not accept the possibility that China would become a major oil dealer, arguing "only an ignorant analyst could join those irresponsible promoters who a decade ago were presenting China as the future Oriental Saudi Arabia".[2]

He made these observations despite the fact that China was the fourth largest oil producer in the world in 1988[3] at the time of his writing and was basically self-reliant in oil until only 1993. However, even Smil had to grudgingly acknowledge the speed of Chinese oil

[1] Smil, V. (1988). *Energy in China's Modernization Advances and Limitation*, pp. 7–8. Armonk, New York/London: East Gate Book ME Sharpe, Inc.

[2] Ibid., p. 8.

[3] Shi, B. (1999). *Zhongguo Shiyou Tianranqi Zhiyuan* (*China's Oil and Natural Gas Resources*), p. 47. Beijing: Shiyou Gongye Chubanshe.

industrial development: "In the mid-1980s China's oil industry clearly ranked amongst the world's largest. After having moved from the twenty-seventh spot worldwide in 1950 to fifth in 1982, it then dropped a bit to seventh place in 1983, but in 1986 it was again the world's fifth largest, just ahead of Mexico."[4] While Smil attributed Daqing's success to chance, the Chinese view on the same subject gravitated around the doctrine of self-reliance.

TERMINOLOGY

The vocabulary of self-reliance in the PRC is represented by various terms such as *ziligengsheng, zigei* or autonomous production (*zixing shengchan*). *Zigei* is re-introduced in the article *Daqing Jingshen, Daqing Ren* (*Daqing Spirit, Daqing Man*) published in the *People's Daily* on 20th April 1964 where the oilfield was revealed to the public at large for the first time. The article touted Daqing's relevance to China's path to oil self-reliance (*shiyou zigei*).[5] Daqing technicians worked under intense political pressures to expand production rapidly using the indigenous method of extraction.[6]

Ziligengsheng was a prominent term in the "*Gongye Xue Daqing* (Industries Learn from Daqing)" campaigns in slogans such as "*ziligengsheng, jiankufendou, pochumixin, jiefangshixiang* (Self-dependence, Strive Hard, Break Superstitions and Liberate Thoughts)".[7] Another example was "getting every enterprise to emulate Taching and

---

[4] Smil, V. (1988), p. 102. While Smil traced China's ascent into the world's major oil-exporting countries to 1982, PRC oil literature cited 1978 as the year of China's emergence as a major oil export player when it surpassed the 100 million tons mark in oil output. (*Source*: Zhang, W. (1999). *Dangdai Zhongguo Youqi Kantan Zhongda Faxian* (*The Important Discoveries of Contemporary China's Oil and Gas Exploration*), p. 4. Beijing: Shiyou Gongye Chubanshe.

[5] Gaimusho Keizaikyoku Keizaitogoka (Japan's Ministry of Foreign Affairs Economics Bureau Economics Statistics Section) (1970), p. 168.

[6] Lieberthal, K. and Oksenberg, M. (1986), p. 162.

[7] Guangdongshen Geming Weiyuanhui Gongshe Bangongshi/Zhengzhibu (The Guangdong Revolutionary Committee Administration and Political Affairs Bureaus) (1973).

work hard and self-reliantly".[8] *Zixing shengchan* seems to be used exclusively by the post-war Taiwanese government to describe the PRC oil industry. Through Daqing, the Taiwanese government admitted in a 1971 restricted government report that China had managed to overcome the label of "oil-impoverished nation (*pinyouguo*)" and "possibly rose to the level of self-provision/self-reliance (*keneng shenzi zigeizizhu de jiecheng*)".[9]

Official publications by the PRC oil industrial press also perpetuated the venerable concept of self-reliance, stressing the need to "proliferate self-reliance (*fayang ziligengsheng*)" and "jolt the strong sense of responsibility of the Chinese people (*zhenzing zhonghua de qianglie zherengan*)" in the Chinese oil industry.[10] The biographical survey of the Chinese oil industry published by the PRC's statistical bureau noted that Daqing seemed to have served its purpose of "instilling patriotic spirit within the Chinese people, establishing self-reliance, display imprints of heroism",[11] etc. Patriotism had historical roots in the Sino-Japanese war.

War in both its forms against the Japanese and the Nationalist shaped the meaning of self-reliance. First, their withdrawal to Yenan (1936–1947) amplified the ideological component of self-reliance. Thereafter, the Communists' rationalistic mobilization of spartan wartime resources had many similarities with the Nationalists. While both received help from external allies during the war (with the Nationalist enjoying greater materiel help from the Americans), self-reliance, however, was integrated more firmly into Communist ideology, especially with the postwar Sino-Soviet split reinforcing it. Cut off

---

[8] Foreign Languages Press (1977), p. 67.

[9] Jingjibu (Ministry of Economic Affairs), Republic of China (1971). *Dalu Feiqu Changkuang Gailan (General View of The Industries in Mainland China) Volume 1[Restricted]*, p. 79. Taiwan: Jingjibu.

[10] Zhongguo Lianyou Gongye (China Oil-Refining Industry) Editorial Team (1989), p. 547.

[11] Guojia Tongjiju Gongjiaoshi (National Statistical Bureau) and Xinhuashe Guoneibu Gongye Bianjishi (Xinhua News Agency National Industries Editorial Department) (1990). *Zhongguo Teda Qiye Zhuanlue (A Brief Biography of China's Extra Large Enterprises)*, p. 13. China: Hualingchubanshe.

from foreign sources of oil with the Sino-Soviet split, a postwar anti-imperialist bent provided continuity for self-reliance and hence the re-applicability of a definitive focus on keeping initiative in one's hands, to develop and master one's domestic resources in order to prevent external powers from targeting one's vulnerabilities. In some ways, this was similar to the Nationalist strategy of withdrawing into the interior to keep war against Japan on their own terms and initiatives. Communist conception of self-reliance traversed the terrain previously traveled by Nationalist renderings of the same concepts.

Severe traumatic experiences with Japanese deprivation through naval boycott during the Pacific War, post-WWII material blockade by the Nationalists during the civil war and Soviet denial of help after the Sino-Soviet split pushed self-reliance to a whole new higher level and intensity, characterized by Smil as "xenophobia". External factors stimulated Chinese impulses towards self-reliance, deprivation influenced its intensity while ideology integrated the concept into Communist developmental ideology.

FOREIGN OPINIONS

The multiplicity of meanings of the term "self-reliance" in the Chinese oil industry is sometimes obscured, ignored or intentionally made amorphous so that terms could be made adaptable and acceptable under different regimes, times, regions and environments. The PRC's *zili gengsheng* policy is in fact an accumulation of such desires for self-reliance in the developmental history of China's oil industry. Literalists defined self-reliance as utilizing domestic instead of foreign ideas and resources.[12] IDE-JETRO's study on the Chinese oil industry cited the 1960s to the 1970s as the period where China adopted the policy of *duli zizhu zili gengsheng* (tzu-li Keng-sheng in Wades Giles) or independent autonomy, self-reliance.[13]

[12] Lee, T. H. (1995), p. 186.

[13] Tatsu, K. (2002), p. 20.

Lieberthal disagrees with such literalists who interpret Chinese self reliance (*zili gengsheng*) to mean total independence.[14] Unlike literal readings of the concept and the vocabulary, Lieberthal argues that self-reliance did not refer exclusively to numerical or quantitative criteria but to "keep initiative in one's own hands".[15] The focus on the means of reducing reliance on others and diversifying one's supply sources, rather than the ends of actual numerical and quantitative self-reliance, is a function of the trauma of Soviet betrayal with the withdrawal of aid and advisors.

Lieberthal also argues that the concept partly arose out of the success of the Long March and the Yanan period[16] where idealized notions of austerity and frugality seemed to have triumphed over adversity. Perhaps, this was reflected in the sheer brute labor used to make the Daqing project possible with the most basic of tools and through sheer steadfast stubbornness in not using any foreign technologies. Following this argumentation, self-reliance was more of a historical experience than an achieved state. In addition, from the economics angle, self-reliance from this viewpoint was made possible by China's abundant labor and capital shortage.[17]

Finally, Lieberthal also associated self-reliance with its strategic dimensions of having self-contained units so that Chinese industrial and agricultural functions could be supported from the most isolated areas of China's interior in the case of a foreign attack. China's vastness and underdeveloped transportation network necessitate self-reliance as well.

Adopting a similar viewpoint as Lieberthal, Leslie Chan saw self-reliance as a form of sheer motivational thinking to overcome odds, "positive thinking and habit of analysis" drawn from Maoist

---

[14] Lieberthal, K. (2004). *Governing China*, p. 77. New York and London: WW Norton & Company.

[15] Downs, E. S. (2000). *China's Quest for Energy Security*, p. 11. California and Virginia: RAND.

[16] Lieberthal, K. (2004), p. 76.

[17] Keith, R. C. (1986). China's Resource Diplomacy and National Energy Policy. In *Energy, Security and Economic Development in East Asia*, Keith, R. C. (ed.), p. 47. NY: St Martin's Press.

thinking.[18] Chan conceptualized self-reliance as a "non-material"[19] incentive to overcome difficulties, much like Lieberthal tracing the same concept back to the Yanan days of overcoming insurmountable difficulties through intangible means of mobilization.

In another perspective, taking on the angle that self-reliance resulted as a response to the impact of external intrusion into China, Kim Woodard postulated that, in the energy industry, self-reliance referred to governmental control over the domestic energy system.[20] Woodard, too, saw the self-reliance policy as an accumulation of over a century's "national humiliation, unification and revolution" and an attempt to "regain its technological and scientific independence and preeminence".[21] She translated *dulizizhu ziligengsheng* as "Independence, self-mastery, relying on oneself, producing more" and abbreviates it to self-reliance.[22] Woodard argued that China's energy development experienced interference from the "intrusion of foreign companies and the governments of foreign countries",[23] a trauma that still dichotomized Chinese conceptions of their developmentalism from Western ideas. The latter prefers to view their past evaluations of Chinese oil potential as underestimations rather than based on ulterior motives.

In the early days of the PRC, negative experience with foreign oil collaboration was reinforced by the Soviet withdrawal of aid and technical help for the industry in 1960, leading to the need to react to the "historical succession" of foreign intrusions, necessitating nationalism to control institute "resource sovereignty"[24] — a phrase repeated as late as Deng's speech to the UN in the 1970s. Woodard argued that, from this historical context, self-reliance refers to

[18] Chan, L.W. (1974), p. 5.

[19] Ibid.

[20] Downs, E. S. (2000), p. 11.

[21] Woodard, K. (1980). *The International Energy Relations of China*, p. xviii. California: Stanford University Press.

[22] Ibid., p. 31.

[23] Ibid., p. 32.

[24] Ibid., p. 33.

"any measure or series of measures that ensures the independent operation of a country's domestic energy system".[25] Thus, resource sovereignty was control over one's energy destiny and autonomous use of fuels.

Proponents of this view saw Mao's ideological focus in self-reliance over foreign technical help as a form of inoculation from infection by foreign ideas. Some went as far as to argue that Chinese humiliation by Western imperialists since the mid-19th century added support to the concept of self-reliance.[26] Extrapolating historically, they pointed out that China was, in fact, more inward-looking during the Maoist era than it was since imperial times as China's percentage of total world exports was only 0.7 percent.[27] A Japanese point of view in JETRO's publication *Chugoku no Sekiyuu to Tenran Gasu* (*China's Oil and Natural Gas*) described China's self-reliance policy as "*hansakokuteki* or half-seclusion-like".[28]

Other variants of "self-reliance" definitions pinpoint the origins of the policy to singular events like the abrupt pullout of Russian advisors and technical help mentioned earlier. The Russian pullout trauma theory is one of the most common explanations and definitions of self-reliance and it is perhaps also accepted officially by the US government through publications from the US Department of Energy. The US Department of Energy Document DOE/IA-0012 prepared by the office of International Affairs in September 1981, for example, noted that "the departure of the Russians kindled a sense of 'self-reliance' which was fueled by the discovery and subsequent development of China's largest oil field, Daqing, in 1959".[29]

Whether it is targeted at the Americans or the Russians, Ronald C. Keith noted that Chinese scholarship has defined self-reliance as a gauge of China's national power — in terms of the "economic ability

[25] Ibid.

[26] Lee, T. H. (1995), p. 186.

[27] Center of International Studies Princeton University (1981). *The Modernization of China*, Rozman, G. (ed.), p. 249. New York and London: The Free Press.

[28] Tatsu, K. (2002), p. 36.

[29] US Department of Energy (1981). *Energy Industries Abroad DOE/IA-0012 September 1981*, p. 239. US: Office of International Affairs.

to sustain a huge growing population and a self-supporting capability for continuous economic growth on the basis of a comparatively low level of development".[30] Following this definition, China's ability to shoulder "protracted strategic burden" whether imposed by the US or by USSR, is consciously seen as proportional to the rate of domestic economic development and national strength from the viewpoint of the Chinese.[31]

For those preferring to see economic autonomy as part of national strength, self-reliance takes the guise of balancing commodity imports and exports or preferably show surplus on the trade account.[32] One way to avoid trade deficits, in the self-reliance worldview, was to depend on domestic resources as much as possible without foreign participation, exchanges or exploitation. In the ideal sense, foreign trade in others words should be as one-way as possible with foreign trade mainly as a way to secure capital, technologies and processed materials.

Ultimately, following a China-centered view, foreign aid, trade or intervention might have been secondary to Chinese priorities enunciated through Mao Zedong's famous 1958 directive which read "self-reliance is primary while striving for foreign assistance is supplementary (*zili gengsheng wei zhu, zhengqu waiyuan wei bu*)".[33] Premier Zhou Enlai further elaborated, due to China's large land mass, population and resources, engaging in international exchange was secondary to the indigenous methods of solving China's problems.[34] Mao ultimately revealed that though "it is necessary to win Soviet aid", "the most important thing is self-reliance".[35]

The Communists' usage of *ziligengsheng* also dates back to the prewar period. Steven Goldstein defines it as "the foreign policy of

[30] Keith, R. C. (1986), p. 18.

[31] Ibid.

[32] Prybyla, J. S. (1978). *The Chinese Economy*, p. 183. Columbia: University of South Carolina Press.

[33] Keith, R. C. (1986), p. 23.

[34] Ibid.

[35] Ibid.

opposition", a tool by which the Communist Party of China (CCP) can influence the actions taken by foreign states.[36] The CCP wanted to maintain autonomy, initiative and bargaining strength in pressuring or negotiating with capitalist governments through the maintenance of an autonomous organizational structure, a military and economic base and an army.[37] In contrast, the CCP saw the Nationalists' weak links with the Chinese masses and emphasis self-interest as being subservient to imperialists and dependent on external help or *wai-lai gengsheng* (*wai-lai kengsheng* in Wades Giles) and led China along the same path.

Through its policy of self-reliance, the CCP proclaimed that it alone has the nationalist credentials to rule China since it sees itself as not being dependent on Anglo-American help and autonomous of Moscow's political fluctuations and therefore was in the best position to decide what was best for China. Following this definition of self-reliance, it has both domestic (self-reliance at individual production units) and international dimensions (self-reliance as a foreign policy strategy). In the 1960s, the international angle of self-reliance applied almost exclusively to weaning away dependence from Moscow after the Sino-Soviet split.

Commentators like Lieberthal had also established some links between prewar and postwar initiatives centering on the institutional construction of self-reliance. For example, US government-affiliated reports studying the Chinese oil industry attributed the origins of institutions supporting the idea of oil self-reliance to Nationalist initiatives like establishing a geology major at Qinghua.[38] "Self-reliance" has also appeared in US diplomatic service reports dating back to the wartime era. For example, in a memoranda dated 9 October 1944 written by US Foreign Service Officer John Stewart Service while on field work in China, it was noted that total mobilization made possible by

---

[36] Goldstein, S. M. (1992). The CCP's Foreign Policy of Opposition 1937–1945. In *China's Bitter Victory, The War with Japan 1937–1945*, Hsiung, J. C. and Levine, S. I. (eds.), p. 114. New York and England: East Gate Book ME Sharpe, Inc.

[37] Ibid.

[38] Lieberthal, K. and Oksenberg, M. (1986), p. 21.

Communist economic, political and social revolutions "has freed them [the Chinese] from feudalistic bonds and given them self-respect, self-reliance and a strong feeling of cooperative group interest".[39] Following this real-time observation, the concept of self-reliance during wartime might be equated with one of the goals of mobilization.

SELF-RELIANCE AND DAQING

The concept of self-reliance reached its zenith in the PRC when the cherished aim of self-reliance was vigorously projected onto all Chinese industries through the "Learn from Daqing" conferences. Daqing-ism meant "getting every enterprise to emulate Taching [Daqing] and work hard and self-reliantly".[40] Self-reliance had evolved to become a value system in Daqing. It embodied and became defined as a national culture through which a collective or communal identity can be constructed and highlighted. The doctrine was freed of its spatial limitations and allowed to blossom extensively. The doctrine of self-reliance also acted as an ordering and bordering ideology within the national imagination against foreign reliance.

In 1960 with the discovery of Daqing, China saw hope for oil self-reliance for the first time. The discovery was vital because most of China's heavy industries (both for civilian and military production) were located in the eastern flank which required the heaviest use of oil.[41] Before the discovery of Daqing, the PRC had to transport oil over vast distances to eastern China but Daqing put an end to that need.[42] Crude oil production attained 6 million tons within less than four years after 1960.[43] This by itself was an amazing feat

---

[39] Department of State (1967). *The China White Paper August 1949 Volume II, Originally Issued as United States Relations with China With Special Reference to the Period 1944–1949 Department of State Publication 3573 Far Eastern Series 30*, p. 566. California: Stanford University Press.

[40] Foreign Languages Press (1977), p. 67.

[41] Yang Jiliang (1999), p. 277.

[42] Ibid.

[43] Wong, J. and Wong, C. K. (1998), p. 12.

given that the entire Chinese oil extraction history from the time when oil was first discovered in China to 1949 at the founding of the PRC was 646,000 tons.[44] Thirteen years after the discovery of China in 1960, China's crude oil output reached 100 million[45] by the time China was ready to export its resources to the outside world with the US recognition of China in 1972 and the open-door policy in 1978.

Through Daqing, the Taiwanese government admitted in a 1971 restricted government report that China had managed to overcome the label of "oil-impoverished nation (*pinyouguo*)" and "possibly rose to the level of self-provision/self-reliance (*keneng shenzhi zigei-hizhu de jiecheng*)".[46] Despite the characterization of the 1958–1978 period as the "lost decades",[47] China, in fact, achieved remarkable progress towards self-reliance in this period in the oil industry. Dependent on oil imports in all of its modern history, the People's Republic of China finally became self-reliant in petroleum production in the mid-1960s, started to export modest amounts in the early 1970s and by the mid-1980s.[48] The PRC whittled down the dependency rate for foreign machinery imports and increasing its self-sufficiency rate from 35 percent in 1953–1957 to 80 percent between 1960–1974.[49] Just as important, China's progress in the oil industry served as a morale booster in the often tumultuous early years of the PRC.

IDEOLOGICAL VALUE

Daqing was a collaborative project. The constellation of revolution and modernity forces produced a deliberate experiment to mobilize two dialectical but key segments of China's industrialization and modernization: the ideological revolutionary teachers and the technocratic

---

[44] Shi, B. (1999), p. 8.

[45] Wong, J. and Wong, C. K. (1998), p. 13.

[46] Jingjibu (Ministry of Economic Affairs), Republic of China (1971), p. 79.

[47] Smil, V. (1976). *China's Energy*, p. xii. NY: Praeger Publishers.

[48] Lieberthal, K. and Oksenberg, M. (1986), p. 151.

[49] Cheng, C. (1976), p. 112.

elites. The Petroleum technocrats saw it as a solution to oil self-reliance, a remedy to reverse China's backwardness in industrialization and a means to overturn China's dependence on foreign oil and technologies, particularly after the Sino-Soviet split. The presence of a huge technological powerhouse neighbour that is hostile towards China explained partly why the modernization forces behind Daqing gathered with such intensity. In addition, China's ideological leaders saw it as a project with potential to harness its mobilizational symbolism and use it as an example of spiritual victory over imperialistic forces and their embargoes and sanctions.

The Daqing movement went on to mobilize the energies of workers, agriculturalists, technocrats, planners in other sectors of the Chinese economy and society. From top down to bottom up, agents of Daqing sought to involve all sections of Chinese society in the project. A variety of organizations and people played a role in the ongoing process of mobilization for oil self-reliance. Daqing literature stated that self-reliance did not just apply to vital industrial process and machineries but also included peripheral functions like haircutting and instituting mutual assistance amongst workers to help them cut one another's hair.[50]

THE CHINA-CENTERED PERSPECTIVE

From the Chinese perspective at the time of Maoist China, the PRC was determined to avoid dependence on foreign oil supplies and expertise and made it known through the mass media. Perhaps, the Chinese did not really have any choice as they were expelled from the bipolar sphere of the West and the Soviet Bloc. Self-reliance was Mao's way of finding a third path (*dasanxianjianshe*)[51] to development away from the bipolar contesting Cold War universes of the West and Soviet Union.

Mass circulation of publications exhorting the merits of learning from Daqing suggested elements of an indigenous feedback loop in

---

[50] Li, C. (1977), p. 83.

[51] Tatsu, K. (2002), p. 34.

self-reliant production. Industrial workers were urged to heighten their recognition of production issues, self-evaluate one's deficiencies in the production chain and work hard to rectify them based on the given conditions (*tigao renshi, zhaochu ziji gongzuochong de cha ju, genju ziji de tiaojian, tichu qieshigexing de cuoshi, nuli gashanqu*).[52] These elements would be part of China's own road to industrialization.

The developmental philosophy of self-reliance is probably aptly summed up in a series of *Radio Peking* programming on the subject of the Daqing oil field in January 1973. The radio broadcast enunciated: "China must not follow the predatory imperialistic ways of oil extraction which might produce quick results but would do long range damage to production. Taking into consideration both present and future interests, the party committee set the principle of operation that would ensure high and stable output over the long run".[53] The mass inculcation of the idea of Daqing and other Chinese oilfields as symbolic reversals of Western-defined Chinese oil poverty was so strong that, even up till 1980, Western visitors were shown and reminded of PRC's oilfields and refineries by Chinese guides who drove home the point that China was once considered "oil poor" by Western geologists and petroleum engineers.[54]

From the China-centered point of view and its conception of oil historicity, since oil was an important component of a modern industrialized economy, failure to extract one's own indigenous source of oil and exhibiting dependence on foreign oil was conceptualized as symptoms of a failed state. The industrial extraction of crude oil was included as part of the relentless global economic race.

[52] Beijing Chubanshe (Beijing Publisher) (1966), Foreword.

[53] US Government Printing Office (1974). Printed for the use of the Committee on Foreign Affairs, Oil and Asian Rivals (Hearings Before the Subcommittee on Asian and Pacific Affairs of the Committee on Foreign Affairs), House of Representatives 93rd Congress First and Second Sessions September 12, 1973; January 30, February 6, 20, and March 6, 1974, p. 46. Washington: US Government Printing Office.

[54] Woodard, K. (1980), p. 32.

CRITICISMS OF CHINESE OIL SELF-RELIANCE

However, not everyone accepted the association of self-reliance with Daqing. Not everyone accepted the Chinese worldview of self-reliance in the oil industry. Vaclav Smil, for example, characterized China's determination in rejecting foreign help as "xenophobic".[55] Wolfgang Bartke who was much less critical of Chinese oil development saw the Chinese doctrine of self-reliance as being compatible with its desire to become a model for developing countries and legitimacy as the protector of the Third World.[56]

Other oil analysts noted that the Chinese tended not to give credit to Soviet aid after the Sino-Soviet split. In the formative years of the PRC, Soviet oil was the lifeline for the fledgling PRC right from the start, with the PRC importing 1 million tons of oil per year.[57] According to Cheng Chu-yuan, between 1959 and 1961, China imported an annual average of three million tons of oil from the USSR.[58] Russian trade figures were lower (see Tables 4.1 and 4.2 below). With vague releases of data for this period, actual figures are probably somewhere in between these two sources. In 1963, after Russian oil supply dried up with the Sino-Soviet split, China turned to Romania for its supplies of oil, importing one million ton in that year itself.[59]

Despite idealized self-reliance, the PRC still needed foreign help with its oil development (see Table 4.3). The importation of oil equipment underlined the limitations to the doctrine. In an attempt to address the equipment deficiency, the PRC built a large number of industrial plants for making oil-related equipment, including drills, rigs

---

[55] Smil, V. (1976), p. 98.

[56] Bartke, W. (1977), p. 26.

[57] Jentleson, B. (1986). *Pipeline Politics*, p. 84. Ithaca and London: Cornell University Press.

[58] Cheng, C. (1976), p. 24.

[59] Ibid.

Table 4.1: China's imports of oil (1,000 tons).

From the Soviet Union

Year	Crude	Kerosene	Diesel	Lubricant	Misc.	Total
1955	378	264	233	72	2	571
1956	397	240	377	74	2	693
1957	380	373	380	95	1	1422
1958	672	333	663	199	1	1836
1959	636	380	557	211	9	2413
1960	568	386	709	212	11	2373
1961	—	512	841	218	6	2902
1962	—	488	378	210	6	1847
1963	—	476	333	137	6	1407
1964	—	139	80	15	1	505
1965	—	2	4	—	—	38

From other countries

Year	Rumania and Albania	Iran	Other Countries	Total
1955	—	0	276	1219
1958	—	0	752	3217
1960	—	199	728	3847
1961	—	199	279	3360
1962	462	199	576	3021
1963	335	199	1055	2989
1964	238	199	1356	2264
1965	237	199	531	1005
1966	235	199	—	474
1967	—	—	—	7
1968	—	—	—	1
1970	—	—	400	400

Taken from *Vneshnya Torgovlia* (Foreign Trade), Moscow, 1966-, as digested in Chen and Au, 1972, p. 332; and various sources as quoted in Chang, 1974, p. 33.
(Park, Choon-ho, *Energy Policies of the World: China* (Newark Delaware; Center for the Study of Marine Policy), 1975, p. 51.)

Table 4.2: Chinese imports of oil and petroleum products from the Soviet Union in ruble terms.

Year	Crude Oil		Petroleum Products	
	Quantity (Million Tons)	Ruble Value (Million)	Quantity (Million Tons)	Ruble Value (Million)
1956	0.3973	59.4	1.3350	284.5
1957	0.3804	56.8	1.4220	304.6
1958	0.6720	59.9	1.8352	309.5
1959	0.6359	12.4	2.4123	93.6
1960	0.5676	10.9	2.3952	90.0

Source: Ajia Tsushinsha (Asia News Agency) (1963). *Chugoku Sangyou Boeki Souran (An Index of China's Industries and Trade)*, p. 104. Japan: Ajia Tsushinsha.

Table 4.3: Imports of oil equipment from the Soviet Union in 1955–1957 (million rubles).

Type of Equipment	Unit of Measure	1955 Quantity	1955 Costs	1956 Quantity	1956 Costs	1957 Quantity	1957 Costs
Marine diesels	Units	305	11.1	180	9.0	62	3.5
Mining equipment	—	—	1.3	—	0.9	—	4.6
Oil drilling equipment	—	—	52.7	—	76.7	—	51.2
Drilling installations	Sets	39	27.2	44	30.9	17	11.8
Rotary turbine drills	Sets	—	—	60	6.7	125	2.4
Chisels	1000 units	5.1	3.1	6.9	6.1	5.8	6.9

Source: Kapelinsky, Y. N. (1959). *Development of the Economy and the Foreign Economic Contracts of the People's Republic of China*, p. 434. NY: CCM Information Corporation.

and their components.[60] In some sectors of equipment needs, Daqing achieved complete self-reliance, for e.g., all screws used at the Daqing oilfield were made by 150 workers in a factory located in the central hamlet.[61]

[60] Ling, H. C. (1975), p. 72.
[61] Bartke, W. (1977), p. 75.

Western observers like H. C. Ling argued that the PRC's claims of introducing methods of "early water injection" and "simultaneous multiple-zone water injection" for the first time in Daqing were exaggerated or untrue.[62] They noted that these techniques had been used in the West and Soviet Union for many years.[63] Even as late as 1990, long-time Chinese oil industry critic Vaclav Smil opined that "in spite of growing imports from the West, much of the industry still has an unmistakable look of the Soviet technologies of the 1950s".[64]

He blamed the exaggerations on the Western media as well: "When China was rediscovered by the Western media, after the Nixon-Kissinger pilgrimage in 1972, numerous apologists for the Maoist regime tried hard to create the image of a country truly apart; an admirable, efficient society dedicated to economic advancement and well-being, a nation of vigorous growth rates, plenty of food, and a smile on everyone's face. And a feat in such startling contrast to post-1973 Western woes, a nation with self-reliant and vigorously expanding energy supplies."[65]

Detractors of Daqing self-reliance perhaps failed to take into account or give due credit to Chinese innovations and adaptations to the local environment, including substitution of manual labor in place of deficiencies. In discussing China's industrial development, Thomas Rawski opined that while analysts may emphasize the role of Soviet models and technicians in industrial design and research development, "reports of independent Chinese progress are not without merit, especially with regard to technical and design modifications needed to operate Soviet processes and equipment".[66]

---

[62] Ling, H. C. (1975), p. 13.

[63] Ibid.

[64] Smil, V. (1990). China's Energy: Advances and Limitations. In *Energy in China*, Desai A. V. (ed.), p. 90. New Delhi: International Development Research Centre and United Nations University.

[65] Smil, V. (1988), p. 3.

[66] Rawski, T. G. (1980), p. 46.

With regards to this point, Wolfgang Bartke had another theory. In his view, even though the USSR provided the Chinese oil industry with technical help, much of their assistance and technologies were imparted in the early years of the PRC before 1960 and had mostly become obsolete by Daqing's time. Thus, he concluded, "In any case, it was by relying on her own resources that China has developed into a modern oil-producing country, and this deserves our highest respect".[67]

Rawski also argued that newly-imported facilities in the 1970s "contributed only marginally to the opening of new oil fields, refineries, pipelines, and port facilities and the expansion of older units".[68] In opposition to Smil's observations of Soviet reliance, Rawski observed that while China had purchased several refinery plants overseas, their combined capacity was responsible for only a tiny segment of the post-1960 (1960s being the era of strict self-reliance) surge in oil production.[69]

Rawski postulated that, despite Romanian and Soviet help, "there can be no doubt that the bulk of the equipment and supplies needed to expand petroleum output from less than 10 million tons annually during the early 1960s to over 90 million tons in 1977 has come from domestic suppliers".[70] For example, more than 40,000 pieces of equipment for the Chinhuangtao-Peking (Qinhuangdao-Beijing) pipeline such as steel pipes, big motors, oil pumps, transformers and auxiliary equipment were made and processed by 240 factories in various parts of China.[71]

The hybridized nature of China's oil industrial makeup and its willingness to draw from an eclectic range of sources, including its own, was perhaps well-summarized in the 1958 guidelines formulated by the Ministry of Petroleum. It advocated a developmental program "to combine foreign and native methods, to plan for comprehensive

---

67 Bartke, W. (1977), p. 12.

68 Rawski, T. G. (1980), p. 64.

69 Ibid., p. 61.

70 Ibid., pp. 61-62.

71 Bartke, W. (1977), p. 35.

utilization of resources, and to strive for self-reliance (in petroleum products)."[72] Older equipment were reused in other ways to optimize their capabilities. For example, in Daqing, a set of well-used equipment originally meant for digging up to 3,000 m was adapted to excavate a 4,500 m deep hole through an indigenously-developed technique.[73] The PRC was able to gradually hone the use of these equipment through their own attempts. In the PRC, wells are seldom dug deeper than 4,000 m but 1978 probably indicated a milestone in this area with a well dug to a depth of 7,175 m.[74]

Other local innovations claimed by the PRC included improved drill bits, a 30 percent lighter small oil-collecting tree to replace the Western version of "Christmas tree" and a solution for transporting Daqing oil that contained high content of paraffin wax.[75] Daqing personnel decided that the Christmas tree type drilling assembly was too clumsy and thus came up with a smaller version that was less than one-third of the old variety and was manned by fewer operators due to its automated functions.[76] PRC sources listed the total number of such innovations at 400.[77] These included 100–200 tons distilling towers that could reach 40 m.[78] Perhaps, the most important contribution that the PRC presented to the global oil industry was its redesign of old Soviet rig designs to come up with a new type of medium-depth power drilling rig that is considered a "major technological breakthrough" by observers in the West.[79]

Through trade fairs and international exchanges, oil innovations were important displays of one's capabilities and rites of passage to laying legitimacy on the oil resources. Chinese indigenous achievements

---

[72] Cheng, C. (1976), p. 6.

[73] Ling, H. C. (1975), p. 147.

[74] Zhu, Y. (1990). Demand, Supply and Economics of Energy in China. In *Energy in China*, Desai A. V. (ed.), p. 19. New Delhi: International Development Research Centre and United Nations University.

[75] Ling, H. C. (1975), p. 131.

[76] Bartke, W. (1977), p. 71.

[77] Ling, H. C. (1975), p. 165.

[78] Bartke, W. (1977), p. 71.

[79] Cheng, C. (1976), p. 118.

were not solely restricted to incremental innovations. Trial and error experiments were encouraged, e.g., Chinese technicians carried out thousands of tests before discovering the optimum water injection variant most suited to the environments of Daqing and other Chinese oilfields.[80] Other than the equipment that was imported, the construction and management of the oilfield was entirely Chinese in makeup.[81] The PRC petroleum research community also claimed a new technique for making catalysts to crack oil as their own.[82] For example, in making sealants, the publication *Bainian Shiyou (100 Years of Petroleum) 1878-2000* published by China's Dangdai Zhongguo Chubanshe in 2002 stated:

> "In May 1962, the oil extraction institution was officially established, headed by Liu Wenzhang and Wan Renfu as vice-head. This was the first unit led by technical personnel at Daqing. From the beginning, they faced difficulties in their work, they constructed wooden huts and tried to self-manufacture their own equipment. Within a short time, the first generation sealant prototype was ready; it could only withstand up to Level 25 atmosphere pressures which was still far from the requirement of 150 atmosphere pressures that was needed. Despite continuous testing and experimentation, the progress was slow. The reason was because they were not able to source for high pressure resistance rubber materials at that time. Kang Shien instructed Liu Wenzhang to confront failure and to locate the systemic factors. Kang said, "Regarding the problem of the rubber materials, you can look for Tang Ke. He could help to solve the problem." Tang Ke was then working at Daqing and he wrote to his comrade-in-arms during the anti-Japanese resistance, Mayor of Harbin Lu Qien, to request the help of a rubber factory in Harbin in solving this problem. In collaboration with this rubber factory and going through 108 rounds of experiments, rubber that could withstand up to atmospheric pressure of 150 was successfully manufactured. Thereafter, with repeated attempts of improvements and attempts, the material eventually was able to resist up to atmospheric pressure of 250. This could satisfy the different requirements at various geo-strata for water injection. In 1964, this was applied at 101 well and 444 geological strata. This was during the

[80] Ling, H. C. (1975), p. 73.

[81] Ibid., p. 52.

[82] Ibid., p. 72.

oilfield's high production period and the sealant product became a basic technique and imprint for future use."[83]

While Soviet help was crucial in the early years of the PRC, a cornerstone in China's own postwar developmental philosophy was to develop the field at a maximum rate and to do so without reliance on foreign technicians, capital and equipment.[84] This policy decision would persist from early 1960 to late 1983.[85] The PRC sought to wean itself off foreign equipment importation gradually. During its First Five-Year Plan, it purchased 351 million rubles (341 million yuan) in oil equipment from the Soviet Union and a small portion of its equipment needs from Romania and East Germany (3.4 percent of total imports).[86] China was only able to manufacture 20–35 percent of its equipment needs for the oil industry in the 1950s.[87] Its capabilities were increased gradually, whittling down the dependency rate for foreign machinery imports and increasing its self-reliance rate from 35 percent in 1953–1957 to 80 percent between 1960–1974.[88]

To challenge the PRC's oil industrial development even further, from the other side of the Cold War divide, the Paris-based Coordinating Committee (COCOM) composed of the US and its allies which controlled exports to communist countries, also did not permit the export of advanced petroleum equipment and technologies to China at that time.[89] Pushed to the brink, Chinese technicians applied technology they had learnt from the Soviet Union, drew upon pertinent articles in American petroleum engineering journals and may have marginally benefited from Romanian assistance to construct their oil industry.[90]

---

[83] Translated from Wen, *et al.* (2002), pp. 127–128.

[84] Lieberthal, K. and Oksenberg, M. (1986), p. 154.

[85] Ibid.

[86] Cheng, C. (1976), p. 109.

[87] Ibid.

[88] Cheng, C. (1976), p. 112.

[89] Lieberthal, K. and Oksenberg, M. (1986), p. 154.

[90] Ibid.

Nevertheless, on the whole, Chinese oil experts and technicians proceeded largely on their own, and there is no evidence that any foreign advisors assisted in any major way in the post-Soviet pullout self-reliant developmental stages of the Chinese oil industry, something agreed amongst observers of the Chinese oil industry including its critics.[91] Lieberthal's account drawn from a report to the US Ministry of Commerce is corroborated by pro-Beijing accounts such as the writing of journalist Alun Falconer who observed real-time that, though 200 Soviet industrial experts arrived in 1949 as instructors, they invariably "work under Chinese direction."[92] Even the Communists' bitter rivals in Taiwan who still referred to the former as "Communist bandits (*gongfei*)" in their official government reports grudgingly observed that the PRC had achieved autonomous production (*zixing shengchan*) in exploration, oil well-digging, extraction, refining and other major oil capabilities in a 1971 restricted report on Chinese industries.[93]

Up to this point, most of the challenges posed for Daqing and the Chinese oil industry as a whole were externally-imposed. The next big obstacle for Daqing would however be the internally-generated challenges unleashed by the Great Proletariat Cultural Revolution.

---

[91] Cheng, C. (1976), p. 13 and Lieberthal, K. and Oksenberg, M. (1986), p. 154.

[92] Falconer, A. (1950). *New China Friend or Foe?* p. 89. Beijing: Foreign Languages Press.

[93] Jingjibu (Ministry of Economic Affairs) (1971), p. 78.

Chapter

5

The Cultural Revolution Interregnum

MAO'S REVERSE COURSE

During the Great Proletariat Cultural Revolution, the distrust of intellectuals (*zhisifenzi*) and experts (*zhuanjia*) were in full play. Mao had never really fully conceptualized how he would treat intellectuals within the Revolution. Judith Shapiro argued that this was a remnant feature left over from the revolution. Two factors led to this state of affairs. First, many intellectuals and technical experts such as those found in the oil industry had supported Communism as a viable path for China to overcome its weakness but the Communist co-opted many of these elites without having a consistent and clarified policy on how to deal with them.[1]

Theoretical debates over the classification of this group of people went on, agonizing whether to classify them as bourgeoisie or proletariat.[2] The amorphous and inconclusive nature of this debate allowed proponents of the Cultural Revolution to attack the Petroleum Faction as bourgeoisie. Thus, what initially started off as an invitation

[1] Shapiro, J. (2001), p. 25.

[2] Ibid.

for technocrats to lead industrial projects in pursuit of China's modernity snowballed into an ideological project to glorify them in an attempt to tackle stagnancy within the cadre membership and bureaucracy but had now regressed into anti-elitist sentiments in the Cultural Revolution.

Michael Gasster highlights this problem of the existence of remnants of the ancient regime amidst a communist China. Gasster, however, saw it as less of a classification problem and more of a problem with centralization. Mao, he argued, was distrustful of centralization since his Yanan days, preferring self-contained guerrilla units but as national development goes underway, divisions and guerilla units became less effective in governing the country. Centralization, which became inevitable, brought along its companions of unavoidable bureaucratization that placed reliance on planners, experts and technocrats.

This, Gasster argued, went against Mao's anti-intellectual beliefs and anti-bourgeoisie stand. Mao saw experts, technicians and planners in industrial megaplexes like Daqing as being drawn mainly from the bourgeoisie class which he felt were contaminated by acquisitiveness and other bourgeois values of the liberal-democratic West that he detested.[3] Mao saw the need for the mobilization of masses to return to the idealized and utopianist anti-elitism days of Yanan. Supporting this line of argument were those in favor of viewing the reversal of fortunes as the Maoist "last stand" against technological foundations of the revolution,[4] represented by complexes like Daqing and modern learning replaced by rural volunteerism and folk studies.

On a more ideological level, some analysts saw this as a manifestation of Mao's broader ideas of contradictions in his understanding of economics. Mao's economic policies according to this school of Chinese oil development had much less to do with economic theory and analysis than with the establishment of a framework for technocrats and economists to operate in.[5] The avoidance of the contradiction of an entrenched technocratic class ruling the mass peasantry

[3] Gasster, M. (1972). *China's Struggle to Modernize*, p. 100. New York: Alfred A. Knopf.

[4] Center of International Studies Princeton University (1981), p. 248.

[5] Chan, L.W. (1974), p. 3.

in the agricultural countryside was in accordance with the resolution of the "three great contradictions"[6] — that of the dichotomy between urban and rural areas, industry and agriculture and mental versus physical labor.

Daqing weighted heavily on urbanization, industrialization and centralized technocratic mental planning and upset the balance in the Maoist idea of contradictions. Contradictions were disfavored in Mao's mind because they create discontent which may lead to peasant unrest.[7] Daqing was beginning to show divergent lifestyles and living standards from the rest of the population, especially the peasantry. Ultimately, Mao placed faith in a society with its constituents fully mobilized and equally engaged in industrial and agricultural work. Daqing was luring people away from this ideal with an industrial bias.

Other analyses saw Daqing's reversal as less of a bureaucratic class or ideological issue and more of personality clashes. Liu Shaoqi, the patron saint of development with his focus on water conservancy projects, grain management[8] and other public systems projects like Daqing, was picked out as the target of vilification during this period. Daqing had depended on Liu's backing but Liu's approach to the revolution was now considered dichotomous to Mao's revolutionary emphasis due to Liu's preference for concentrating on local issues like developmental projects and he was comfortable with the application of specialized knowledge like economics and social sciences as well as science and technology.[9]

In comparison, Mao seemed to be more interested in international and global issues including international politics and economics and was more eclectic in his pet interests, far more wide-ranging than local developmental projects like Liu.[10] Liu's personal philosophy was keen on associating efficiency with equality and order with

[6] Ibid.

[7] Ibid.

[8] Dittmer, L. (1974), p. 207.

[9] Ibid., pp. 207 and 288.

[10] Ibid., p. 207.

revolution,[11] giving him a nice fit with technocracy. Moreover, organization and efficiency were what Daqing represented. However, in Mao's eyes, this was seen to be an overemphasis on organization at the expense of ideological development and insensitivity towards class boundary differences. Liu's willingness to integrate managerial classes, engineers, scientists and technical personnel, a large portion of these being non-Party individuals, into a united Communist front antagonized Mao who was not keen to see the growth of a new class based on the ownership of material, human and technocratic assets.[12] Mao saw the potential for the class to alienate itself from the masses and become tyrannical or elitist, in his words a "tutorial" relationship to the masses.[13]

Although both Mao and Liu saw merits in utilizing industrial models, Liu was far more cautious, preferring controlled experimentation with models on a small scale to prevent things from spinning out of control while Mao, on the other hand, favored things on a grand scale with wide application of slogans, policies and the selection of an ideal model for full-scale emulation.[14] To Mao, Daqing started to reek of Liu's influence, especially what Mao classified as Liu's "economism" which utilized material benefits and capitalistic management to enhance Daqing's success.[15] Ironically, in Mao's eyes and paranoia, if Daqing succeeded, it would destabilize Mao's philosophy of self-reliance and overcoming adversities through stubborn persistence and may prove therefore that Liu's economic pragmatism was more conducive for China's modernization goals.[16] In other words, Daqing's success became a threat.

In Mao's eyes, Daqing was capable of showcasing Liu's ideological alternative, never mind that the model status of the facility was once personally encouraged by Mao himself. Mao, who was still hurting from dissatisfactions with his policies in the Great Leap — having

[11] Ibid., p. 285.

[12] Ibid.

[13] Ibid.

[14] Chan, L.W. (1974), p. 5.

[15] Ibid., p. 14.

[16] Ibid.

experienced personal attacks starting with General Peng Dehuai's personal letter of criticism forwarded to him and his humiliation from having to abdicate the head of state position to Liu Shaoqi — began to see politics in shades of black and white. Jonathan Spence described this dichotomy as one between those who were truly "red" — Maoist orthodoxy and faith in the masses — and those who had specific technocratic expertise in scientific planning or bureaucratic procedures.[17] Daqing was caught in this polemic and dialectic tension and, because of the nature of the project and its planners, it became associated with non-orthodoxy.

The constellation of elite leaders that held Daqing together began to fall apart. Red Guards then proceeded to target Liu's allies, accusing Yu of making Daqing a "sham" model and asserted that the oil field's management ideology had in fact been a good deal less egalitarian and proletariat than what official propaganda had made it out.[18] The Gang of Four launched some of the most virulent attack on the oil facility, calling it bourgeois. In Zhang Chun-qiao's (a member of the Gang of Four) view, instead of efficient and rapid industrialization, "socialist running behind schedule is preferable to a capitalist running on schedule".[19] Daqing was demonized as the destroyer of egalitarianism. Technocratically-led industrialism and its association with individuals trained in elite prewar and postwar institutions clashed with the evocations of an imagined proletariat past bereft of specialist elitism. Yu and other developers of Daqing came under severe attack and were replaced by a new set of officials in charge. The density of technocrats trained with specialist skills within the Petroleum Faction made it a prominent target of attack.

Much later, Kang Shien, a receptor of criticisms during the Cultural Revolution, rebutted the Gang of Four's charges of differentiation between Daqing workers and its leaders. He cited many examples including the fact that the late Premier Zhou Enlai, an object of attack

[17] Spence, J. (1999). *Mao Zedong*, p. 153. New York: Lipper/Viking Book.

[18] Lieberthal, K. and Oksenberg, M. (1986), p. 22.

[19] Wu, T. (1983). *Lin Biao and the Gang of Four*, p. 181. Carbondale and Edwardsville: Southern Illinois University Press.

during the Cultural Revolution, worked and lived amongst workers under the same conditions, including shaking grease-filled hands of Daqing's workers, working late nights with them and constantly caring and asking about workers' welfare.[20] Kang also revealed how Zhou forbade fine grains (he only allowed rough grains like *gaoliang*) and alcohol for meals at Daqing and insisted that only Daqing's own homegrown vegetables like carrots can be used for his dinner table.[21] Backing up this view, contemporary PRC oil literature also argued that other supposedly bourgeoisie personnel in Daqing like university professors worked classlessly along with other field workers, consolidating the latter's work experience and improving technical skills.[22]

However, like many mass movements, once set in motion, the Cultural Revolution developed a life of its own and the masses that drove it were no longer as responsive to restraining forces. Targets of heterodoxy charges and public criticisms slowly became calls for public enemies to be purged and eliminated. The campaigns targeted functional specialists, a label which many of the technocrats fit. Once a Petroleum Faction and Daqing pioneer was targeted, the rest fell like dominoes to the same charges. The Cultural Revolution became an exercise in the rehabilitation of non-entrenched industrial proletariat through social revolution on a grand scale, perhaps unlike anything envisioned before. The Petroleum Faction was in the way of this exercise.

Daqing-ism was more concerned about a production-oriented technological and industrial future while the Cultural Revolution was more concerned with turning the clock back to a more egalitarian non-elitist, non-technocrat past or status quo that employed ideological instead of technological language as an alternative modernity. Daqing did not fit into Mao's normative appeal for the de-emphasis

[20] Kang, S. (1992). Huainian Jignaide Zhou Enlai Tongzhi (Reminiscing the Beloved Comrade Zhou Enlai). In *Jiannan Chuangye Zhongguo Shiyou Gongye Dierji* (*The Difficulties of Starting an Industry: The Chinese Oil Industry Series Two*), Jing, Z. (ed.), pp. 2 and 5. Beijing: Shiyou Gongye Chubanshe.

[21] Ibid., p. 7.

[22] Zhang, W. (1999), p. 268.

of material incentives. Mao was suppressing the Daqing industrial story supported by conservative ideologues' self-molded role as the guardians of orthodoxy.

Daqing's czars like Kang Shien and Yu Qiuli came under severe attack, particularly for the priority they allegedly attached to production and expertise. Yu's allies were labeled as his henchmen who, along with all other disgraced ministerial bureaucrats, were accused of being collaborators of Liu Shaoqi and Deng Xiaoping. What was a boon in having Liu as the patron of the Daqing project became a bane during the Cultural Revolution because Liu became Mao's number one enemy. Liu clashed with Mao over a number of issues including the extent of private enterprise which Mao coined as "revisionism".[23] Mao then mobilized the 516 group of Red Guards to override the Communist Party apparatus controlled by Liu and rescinded Liu's status as his heir apparent in 1966.[24]

Daqing's leaders were isolated for intense criticism. Out of 17 of Daqing's top leaders, 16 were criticized and, out of those criticized, 12 were accused of being "traitors (*pantu*)" and "capitalist roaders (*zouzhipai*)" and were locked in cattle shacks/prisons (*niu peng*).[25] For example, Kang Shien was accused of being an ally of Liu Shaoqi and Deng Xiaoping and was purged in May 1967.[26] As attacks intensified, even Deng's mentor, the venerable Zhou Enlai, was accused of being the leader of the "foreign affairs faction (*yangwu pai*)" that promoted "slavish comprador philosophy" to turn China into a "raw material base" for foreign capital much later in 1976.[27] Kang was an easy target as he had been criticized before as a "bourgeois individual" in the "Three Anti-Campaign" early on in August 1952.[28] He reeked of non-proletarianism. Zhang Zhen (Wades-Giles: Chang Chen), a link between China's oil industry and foreign technical cooperation, was

---

[23] Alexander, G. (1973). *The Invisible China: The Overseas Chinese and the Politics of Southeast Asia*, p. 94. New York: Macmillan.

[24] Ibid.

[25] Kang, S. (1992), p. 11.

[26] Bartke, W. (1977), p. 123.

[27] Keith, R. C. (1986), p. 28.

[28] Bartke, W. (1977), p. 122.

purged in 1967.[29] The Vice-ministers connected with the energy industries were particularly vulnerable. Li Yilin (Wades-Giles: Li Yi-lin), appointed vice-minister for the chemical industry in 1964, disappeared from the public.[30] Sun Jingwen (Sun Ching-wen), appointed vice-minister for the petroleum industry in September 1959, was removed in that fateful year.[31]

The political fates that Yu and Kang met soon extended to Daqing. Daqing ceased to receive national praise in early 1967 and lost its status as a national model until early 1969.[32] In 1966, some units at Daqing started working on a six-hour day schedule to allow workers to devote more time to revolutionary activities in the Cultural Revolution.[33] It was also reported in the 1 October edition of *Hongqi* (*Red Flag*) that Daqing workers "have written several thousand big character posters, dragged out the small handful of rightists who are anti-Party, anti-socialist, and opposed to the thought of Mao Zedong, and won a major victory in the great cultural revolution."[34] Model worker Ironman Wang Jingxi was criticized, beaten, paraded and accused of being a "fake model worker, a landowner and Nationalist (*Jiadianxing, dizhu*, Guomindang)" with over 300 technicians and management staff members in the drilling and extraction as well as industrial functions waylaid under different accusations.[35] By the end of 1966, 6000 units (*ganbu*) throughout the oilfield were criticized, making up almost 90 percent of the total number of units in the oilfield.[36]

In reaction to workers' discontent, the Daqing Party Committee dispensed bonuses and salary advancements to workers and encouraged them to travel to Beijing directly to voice their grievances.[37]

[29] Ibid., p. 123.

[30] Ibid., p. 124.

[31] Ibid.

[32] Lieberthal, K. and Oksenberg, M. (1986), p. 174.

[33] Chan, L.W. (1974), p. 11.

[34] Ibid.

[35] Kang, S. (1992), p. 11.

[36] Ibid., pp. 11 and 12.

[37] Chan, L.W. (1974), p. 12.

They did and Japanese newspapers reported that Premier Zhou Enlai met them on 10 January 1967 who, in his counterattack of the Cultural Revolutionaries, issued a statement denouncing the Daqing Party Committee leaders for instigating the workers to leave production at Daqing and instead travel to Beijing to "exchange revolutionary experiences."[38] Supporting Zhou's counterattack, a news report emerged in the New China News Agency (NCNA) that Daqing party leaders had erroneously forwarded supplementary wages, subsidies and other welfare benefits to the workers which undermined the de-emphasis of materialism in the Cultural Revolution even though the workers later returned these fringe benefits.[39]

One view put forward by Leslie Chan was that discontent arose from tensions created by a dual track system at Daqing. Because both the municipality and the oilfield were under Daqing's administrative jurisdiction, Daqing had two types of workers: the worker-peasant system consisting mainly of new workers in agriculture and other supporting industries, and veteran workers who worked full-time in the oilfield. Because the latter managed the technical and priority tasks, they were paid substantially higher salaries than those workers in the supporting industries since the worker-peasants were only paid work points when they are in the oilfield during off-peak seasons in their supporting jobs.[40] Work points given to the worker-peasants were on the average less than one-third of the full-time veteran oil workers' wages.[41] Attacks by disgruntled workers on Daqing mounted until post-Cultural Revolution statements blamed such ill-advised worker management on operatives within the Daqing party leadership installed by Liu Shaoqi after his visit to the oilfield in the early 1960s.

Intensifying in the severity of accusations leveled on Daqing and the Petroleum Faction, the personalities behind the attacks were also increasingly located in the elite stratum of the PRC communist party hierarchy.

---

[38] Ibid.

[39] Ibid.

[40] Ibid., p. 13.

[41] Ibid.

Red Guard publications indicated that Jiang Qing, Mao's wife and prominent leader in the Cultural Revolution, had personally admonished Daqing representatives of the movement for not criticizing Yu Qiuli, Minister of Petroleum and oil industry czar in China.[42] Yu was accused of being anti-Mao and of nepotism by appointing his close circle to posts at Daqing and, consequently, the movement was opposed to the veteran cadres appointed to positions at the oilfield.[43]

Even the biographical film made during the euphoric days of Daqing, *Pioneers*, was heavily criticized by the Gang of Four, the leading elements during the Cultural Revolution. The film was made at the Daqing oilfield in early 1975 without approval from Jiang Qing, one of the Gang of Four members and perhaps the most influential ideologue, who consequently drummed up 10 charges against the film.[44] The other Gang of Four member, Yao Wenyuan, accused the film of "white-washing" Liu Shaoqi's crime.[45] *Pioneer*'s relegation to the rubbish heap of Chinese revolutionary history was prevented only by a timely note from Chairman Mao who apparently favored the film.[46] Similarly, the Gang of Four also used their influence and stalled the production of *Battle Song of Taching*, a project initiated by Premier Zhou Enlai.[47]

SHELTER FROM THE STORM

In this political turmoil, the Petroleum Faction was concerned about seeking protection and rising out the storm. Fortunately, Zhou Enlai played a major role in protecting Yu Qiuli from humiliating persecution and incarceration by the Red Guards by arguing that Yu enjoyed Mao's confidence.[48] When Yu was put up for criticisms on

[42] Ibid., p. 15.

[43] Ibid., p. 13.

[44] Wu, T. (1977), p. 51.

[45] Foreign Languages Press (1977), p. 51.

[46] Ibid.

[47] Ibid., p. 52.

[48] Lieberthal, K. and Oksenberg, M. (1986), p. 67.

7 January 1967, Premier Zhou on behalf of Chairman Mao, convened a large meeting at the workers' stadium in Beijing (*Beijing Gongren Tiyuguan*) for oil and national planning personnel (*Shiyou xitong he Guojia Jiwei*) where he delivered a long speech that conveyed Mao's wishes to protect Yu Qiuli through the coded language of "*yipi erbao* (criticize but protect)".[49]

Zhou threaded the middle line, explaining to the gathering that, while it may be true that Yu had committed mistakes including arrogance, lack of humility and democratic decision-making in work (*gongzhuozhong jiaoaole, bunamu qianxu, minzu zhuofeng bugou*), Yu had his results and contributions, thus earning Mao's protection.[50] In addition, Yu had personal ties within the People's Liberation Army (PLA) that were rivals of the Cultural Revolutionary network led by Lin Biao (a leader of the Red Guards).[51]

Yu Qiuli was promoted to Lieutenant General in 1955[52] and was able to make use of his rank for his own personal protection as well as provide security for the oil facilities. As a result, MPI and Daqing were protected by PLA, particularly its Logistics Department[53] which played a prominent leadership role in preventing total decimation of the industry. Several thousand PLA troops were stationed in Daqing in February 1967 and remained there until spring 1971.[54] By late 1967, they had provided security for the oilfield and insulated it from the political turmoil in China. The military personnel, drawn mainly from the Shenyang and Heilongjiang military districts, assumed administrative responsibilities for the facilities.[55] Besides being a force for order, the military had its own self-interests in seeing that their petroleum supplies were not disrupted as their

---

[49] Wen, *et al.* (2002), p. 197.

[50] Ibid., p. 198.

[51] Lieberthal, K. and Oksenberg, M. (1986), p. 67.

[52] PLA Figures (5 May 2004). *PLA Daily* website http://64.233.161.104/search?q=cache:Nso0okcSdzwJ:english.pladaily.com.cn/special/figures/zj/yql.htm+Daqing+PLA&hl=en

[53] Lieberthal, K. and Oksenberg, M. (1986), p. 67.

[54] Ibid., p. 175.

[55] Ibid.

dependence on the resource greatly increased along with their mechanization program.[56]

In August 1967, antagonisms between the PLA and the Red Guard revolutionaries became full-blown conflict at Daqing. Japanese media reported that the PLA had formed alliances with workers supported by local Party leaders to resist the Cultural Revolution.[57] They were led by Liu Feng-mei, head of the district's Military Control Commission, who mobilized 10,000 anti-Cultural Revolution conservatives from Daqing and PLA supervisors to attack the Red Guards and maintain order and production at Daqing.[58] In autumn 1967, Mao gave his blessings to the PLA by denouncing any attacks from advocates of the Cultural Revolution targeted at the military and, by 16 December 1967, a semblance of order was restored with PLA units mobilized for oil production.[59]

Despite the protective efforts of the anti-Cultural Revolution factions, Daqing was still depleted of able-bodied men. Military and regular engineers and technicians at Daqing kept production going and filled in the vacancies left behind by 10,000 Chinese workers who had gone to Beijing to participate in the revolutionary rallies.[60] The detachment of PLA troops associated with Daqing was later given the affectionate nickname of the "Hard-boned Sixth Company".[61] In general, therefore, it appears that MPI did not suffer as severely during the Revolution and its aftermath as most other ministries. Internally, the MPI and the Petroleum Faction also enjoyed great cohesion which prevented the Revolution from preying on intense factional strife that plagued other ministries.

On hindsight, the energy bureaucracy also acted as a refuge for personalities groomed by the energy bureaucracy to become China's future leaders, like Li Peng. He was promoted within the Petroleum

---

[56] Lee, T. H. (1995), p. 70.

[57] Chan, L. W. (1974), p. 13.

[58] Ibid.

[59] Ibid., pp. 13–14.

[60] Ling, H. C. (1975), pp. 14 and 128.

[61] Foreign Languages Press (1977), p. 33.

Faction to become the minister of electrical power in 1979 while serving as an expert on energy issues within the faction.[62] Li escaped persecution during the Cultural Revolution because he was placed in charge of Beijing's power supply, ensuring his preservation to become the future acting premier in late November 1987.[63]

Aside from external protection and military allies, internally within the organization, MPI's newness, esprit de corps arising from the proven track record in industrial successes as well as homogeneity of its technocratic personnel also gave it a united front that made it less vulnerable to Red Guard attacks.[64] According to Kang Shien, even after being criticized during the day time, many veteran oilfield workers at Daqing moved their luggage to the oil wells and continued working day and night to keep production going.[65]

Similarly, supervisors and leaders of various units who received criticisms in the day turned up at night to continue directing production.[66] The basic outlook amongst the oil personnel was that life and production went on as per normal. Though the MPI still suffered from the Cultural Revolution, because it proved to be more cohesive, it was able to recover from the turmoil of that period with greater rapidity. The Petroleum Faction's military links, powerful patronage and internal unity saw it through countless and chronically uncertain times and offered Daqing and the oil industry an enviable stability.

Daqing as a technocratic project was subordinated to Mao's greater ideological project for China. Political and ideological ideas about Daqing shaped its existence, directing the course of its progression and determining its developmental logic. The trajectory of Daqing transformed from that of a centerpiece model unit to a reactionary counter-example. Its technocratic leaders were deposed quickly and would have been sacrificed if not for the intervention

---

[62] Spence, J. (1999), p. 688.

[63] Ibid.

[64] Lieberthal, K. and Oksenberg, M. (1986), p. 67.

[65] Kang, S. (1992), p. 13.

[66] Wen, *et al.* (2002), p. 197.

of moderate leaders like Zhou and the timely help of another hierarchical and effective organization — the military.

Restraint on the part of top leaders like Zhou and the military — an organ fiercely loyal to the top echelons of the Communist Party indicated contradictory and contesting concepts of technocratic modernization in Mao's thinking. During the Cultural Revolution, Maoist ideology disagreed with the entrenchment of technocrats hitherto represented by the much-vaunted successes of Daqing planners but, yet, restraint in advocating their complete elimination meant that the technocracy could not be dismissed without risking some form of regression in China's industrial progression. The ideologues could not push forward China's self-strengthening and socialist path to modernization without the expert technical knowledge of the planners perceived as having bourgeois roots; each was dependent on the other. Both saw heavy industrialization as a common inoculation for an uncertain age characterized by China's isolation from Cold War bipolarity on both sides of the divide.

Herein lay a contradiction in the political makeup of Daqing represented by the Maoist ideologue's simultaneous suppression and mobilization of technocrats. The destructiveness of the rupture between them during the Cultural Revolution, both in terms of institutions and individual personalities, highlighted the inherent contradiction of industry-building in China and ultimately underlined the fact that coalitions of ideologically-incompatible and economic structurally-differentiated entities were inherently unstable.

RESTORATION

As the Cultural Revolution was contained by moderate forces, Daqing crept back slowly into the ideological limelight. This process began a little earlier than what most Western analysts determined. As early as mid-1969, formerly purged Daqing cadres, many of whom were veterans, were being reinstated to their posts at the oilfield and this once again brought back the emphasis on production leading to revitalized production in 1970 (20 million metric tons) and 1971 (13–15 million tons).[67] In 1971, an attractively-designed book *Daqingren de Gushi* (*Story of the People at Daqing*) put together by *Daqing Youtian Gongren Xiezhuozu* (The Writers' Team for Daqing) was published by Shanghai Renmin Chubanshe (Shanghai People's Publishing House).

Daqing was once again re-associated with Chairman Mao. In ideological jargon, Daqing was raised as a red flag (*yimian hongqi*) in Mao's motivation and the oilfield was said to have been developed along the lines of Mao's classless revolutionary path (*wuchanjieji geming luxian fazhan gongye de daolu*) while the slogan "*Gongye Xue Daqing* (Industry Learn from Daqing)" was revived.[68] Interestingly, the two words "*zuageming, chushengchan* (grasp the revolution, encourage production)" were set in bold in the foreword, implying that production was once again placed on the same pedestal as the revolution.[69] The realization of economic stagnation after the fervor of the revolution was beginning to dawn on Mao and his top planners. On the page following the foreword, a strategically-selected Mao thought was quoted which stressed the "will and capabilities of the Chinese people in catching up with the developed world (*zhongguorenmin you zhiqi, younengli, yiding yaozai buyuan de jianglai, ganshang he chaoguo shijie xianjin shuiping*)".[70]

Geographically, the message from the center needed to be disseminated. Regional conferences aimed at reviving the Learn from Daqing movement was carried out as early as 1973 in regional formats like the *Quanshen Gongyexue Daqing Huiyi* (All-Provincial Learn from Daqing Conference) organized by the Chinese Communist Party Guangdong Provincial Committee. The conference re-propagated the idea of broad education (*guangyu*) in Ironman Wang-style team

[67] Chan, L.W. (1974), p. 14.

[68] *Daqing Youtian Gongren Xiezhuozu* (The Writers' Team for Daqing) (1971), unpaginated foreword.

[69] Ibid.

[70] Ibid., unpaginated.

organization.[71] Another purpose of the conference was to re-proliferate Daqing-style industries and Ironman Wang-style "advanced talents (*xianjing rencai*)".[72] Indoctrination of Ironman Wang emulation was reinforced with interventionist fervor into personal lives and encouraged at other Chinese industries. At the conference, one delegation proposed that veteran workers were more likely to appreciate the contrast between "Old China's societal hardship (*jiushehui de kunanrizi*)" and "New China's societal fortunate lives (*xinshehui de xingfushengjuo*)".[73]

In addition, younger workers were also thought to enigmatically possess the quality of reception of new things with ease but lacked the training of practicality.[74] In other words, younger workers were cast in the light of immature and impressionable individuals who needed the guidance of their seniors and this did not include only their own family members. Like evangelists, senior veteran workers at other mines were asked to visit the families of younger workers within a 100 or a 1,000 miles (*baili jiafang, qianli jiafang*) to encourage family members to participate in ideological indoctrination campaigns.[75] In one case, the parents of a homesick young worker were invited to the mine to participate in an indoctrination program that eventually succeeded in turning out an outstanding demolition expert.[76] Once again, Daqing-ism was poised to penetrate the personal spheres of industrial workers as well as their families.

Publications exhorting Daqing also began to reappear subtly in regional ideological publications in the same year. For example, the *Guangdong Renmin Chubanshe* (Guangdong's People's Publishing Bureau) was endorsed by the *Guangdongshe Geming Weiyuanhui Gongjiao Bangongshe/Zhengzhibu* (The Guangdong Revolutionary

[71] Guangdongshen Geming Weiyuanhui Gongshe Bangongshi/Zhengzhibu (The Guangdong Revolutionary Committee Administration and Political Affairs Bureaus) (1973), unpaginated foreword.

[72] Ibid., p. 1.

[73] Ibid., p. 57.

[74] Ibid., p. 145.

[75] Ibid., p. 23.

[76] Ibid.

Committee Administration and Political Affairs Bureaus) to distribute their publication "*Zoudaqingde Daolu Bandaqingshi Qiye (Walk the Path of Daqing and Carry Out Daqing-style Industries)*". Mao's quotes (*Maoyulu*) "*gongye xue Daqing* (Industries Learn from Daqing)" and "*ziligengsheng, jiankufendou, pochumixin, jiefang-shixiang* (Self-dependence, Strive Hard, Break Superstitions and Liberate Thoughts)" were back in vogue.[77] Self-reliance was a virtue highlighted in submissions such as that from Guangzhou Heavy Machinery (*Guangzhou Zhongxing Jiqichang*) which became bashful in asking for governments for help or handouts and instead learnt to manufacture many types of heavy machinery on their own without external help[78] like the reinstated Daqing.

The emphasis placed on the working class in Daqing complied with the need to symbolically link its development with the proletariat element highlighted in the Cultural Revolution while pragmatically re-positioning Daqing-associated industrial development as a main priority in restoration of the economy in the waning years of the Cultural Revolution. The story of Ironman Wang was recast in this light. This time, the accent was not placed on record-breaking feats or production breakthroughs but on his ironclad commitment to the proletariat masses ("*buyao tuoli qunzhong* (not leave the masses)", "*xinbuli qunzhong* (not to abandon concern for the masses)".[79]

This idea was a post-Cultural Revolution ideal of mixed ideological and technical advancements to bring about material progress in China's revolution. One was incomplete without the other and this was the conclusion reached by a Jiangsu factory which regretted the relaxing of ideological education, leading to a serious industrial accident.[80] This finding was presented in a March 1973 All-Provincial

---

[77] Ibid., unpaginated.

[78] Ibid., p. 70.

[79] *Daqing Youtian Gongren Xiezhuozu* (The Writers' Team for Daqing) (1971), p. 1.

[80] Guangdongshen Geming Weiyuanhui Gongshe Bangongshi/Zhengzhibu (The Guangdong Revolutionary Committee Administration and Political Affairs Bureaus) (1973), p. 131.

Industries Learn from Daqing conference organized by the Committee of the Chinese Communist Party of Guangdong province. The apparent solution to this was to internalize a sense of self-awareness among the workers to follow operational rules established by ideological principles.

As the restoration of the Petroleum Faction, Daqing and Daqingism turned full swing, Post-Cultural Revolution literature was primed for a fierce attack on the Gang of Four. The Gang of Four was accused of splittist attitude, creating disunity amongst the workers by calling Daqing's achievement a "hoax (*jiade*)".[81] Lost in the ideological deconstruction and dismantling of Daqing during the Cultural Revolution, folk symbols such as Ironman Wang Jingxi's exaltations were brought back to life: "Daqing is Mao's Daqing, it is the Daqing of the Chinese people, whoever opposes Mao Zedong, whoever smears Daqing's red flag, we will meet him/her with a fist".[82] Technocrats were also rehabilitated by valuing their experience (*jingyan*) and expert opinion (*zhuanjia*), making both elements just as important as ideology.

The Cultural Revolution's successful decimation of technocratic contributions to industrial development despite Mao-backed ideological campaigns to urge others to learn from the Daqing technocracy demonstrated that if ideological campaigns were carried out mechanistically, it could backfire. Elitism, often an angle of attack against Daqing technocracy and industrial exemplification during the Cultural Revolution, was carefully routed to not emerge as a problem again. The so-called award-mania (*jiangjin zhidu*) including technocratic impulses to seek state recognitions for its role in increasing production or other such forms of materialistic yearnings were "disapproved of by the people (*qunzhong ye bu zhancheng gaojiangjin*)".[83]

---

[81] Song, Z. (1977). Gaoju Mao Zedong de Weida Qizhi, Zou Woguo Zhiji Gongye (Raise the Majestic Flag of Mao Zedong, Walk the Path of Our Indigenous Industries. In *Gongye Zhanxian de Xianyan Hongqi* (*The Brightly-Colored Red Flag of the Industrial Battlefront*), p. 12. China: Renminchubanshe.

[82] Ibid., p. 12.

[83] Ibid., p. 45.

Instead, Daqing was a project for the masses, a career in improving the welfare of the people and raising the standard of living for the people and a way out through self-dependency.[84] Deng Xiaoping eventually restored the policy of workers' welfare in 1978 when he was shocked by the spartan living conditions at Daqing — its sparsely furnished living quarters and the absence of carpet and sofa.[85] Deng also removed existing prohibitions on welfare spending and directed the authorities to reshape Daqing into a "garden city (*huayuanban meilide chengshi*)".[86]

Grassroots activism was also emphasized. Cadre members in the workforce who had not performed adequate grassroots work were urged to "make up for it (*buke*)".[87] Daqing's leading cadres in its long-standing Committee boasted of people from the grassroots and included model soldiers and workers. Even at the factory level committees, 154 cadres with grassroots experience and model military status were also picked to fill in the positions.[88] Technocracy, scientific rationality and technical expertise would have to co-exist with post-Cultural Revolution criterion.

In 1976, restoration was also extended to cultural life in Daqing. In the latter part of the 1970s, utilitarian items like enamel wares, metallic kitchenware coated with a layer of enamel, made by state-owned companies like Reservoir Brand were decorated with Daqing motifs again and mass-manufactured in production lines like 305P-106. The art on the enamel wares thread a cautious line between Cultural Revolution representation like red flags sitting atop oil rigs and a post-Revolution normalcy by having bourgeosie English roses to grace the foreground with the oilfield fading into the background, softening the masculine image of the industrial complex. Because such wares were extensively circulated among the masses as well as exported overseas to customers that included the overseas

---

[84] Ibid., p. 45.

[85] Chen, D. K. (1994), p. 128.

[86] Ibid.

[87] Song, Z. (1977), p. 47.

[88] Ibid., p. 46.

Chinese, they spread the news that Daqing was re-validated again in the end-days of the Revolution. By using these wares, people were reminded that Daqing was back in business.

The *Daqing Wenhua Yishuguan* (Daqing Arts and Culture Museum) published a collection of artistic works under the title of *Daqing Suxie Xuanji (Selected Works of Daqing Sketches)* depicting life restored to normality in Daqing. The book's foremost printed text continued to highlight Chairman Mao's teachings, perhaps a cautious move in the immediate aftermath of the Cultural Revolution. It exhorted the important need for artists and culturalists to return to the "roots of the masses (*bixu dao qunzhong zhong*)" and "mingle with the peasantry and workers wholeheartedly and unconditionally on a long term basis (*bixu changqide wutiaojiande quanxin-quanyide dao gongnongbing qunzhong zhongqu*)": the masses, peasantry and workers were described as the largest scale and richest source of inspiration for the arts.[89]

As a sure sign of Daqing's return to favor, the foreword of the compilation equated Daqing with the leading red flag in China's industrialization and in the thinking of Chairman Mao and, after the classless Cultural Revolution (*wuchan jieji Wenhuadageming*), the red flag flies even brighter (*zhemianqi gengjia xianyan*).[90] The condemnation of Daqing and its operators were now forgotten even in the realm of Daqing arts, connoting continuity with the time of Daqing's discovery when Chairman Mao had praised the oilfield as a model for all other enterprises. Mao himself was re-established as the revolutionary guiding light (*geming luxiande zhiyingxia*) behind Daqing's workers and his leadership was now re-credited with re-instilling scientific rationality amongst the workers (*kexue shiyan*).[91]

Daqing was re-instated as a national benchmark once again. In the Speech by Vice Chairman Comrade Ye Jianying at the National

---

[89] Daqing Wenhua Yishuguan (Daqing Arts and Culture Museum) (1976). *Daqing Suxie Xuanji (Selected Works of Daqing Sketches)*. Heilongjiang: Heilongjiang Renmin Chubanshe.

[90] Ibid.

[91] Ibid.

Chinese Communist Party Central Committee Learn from Daqing Conference in 1977, delegates were urged to evaluate the "gap (*chaju*)" between their units and Daqing and then "in learning from Daqing, employ Daqing's spirit, ideas, policies to eradicate the gap (*Xue Daqing, jiuyaozao zhiji danwei dong Daqing de juli, beingqie yaoyong Daqingren de jingshen, xiang banfa, dingcuoshi, xiaomie juli*)".[92] A new ideological innovation in this period was that the process of benchmarking one's unit against Daqing would become never-ending in perpetuating the process of edging close to the benchmark (*yinggai kandao, jiudejuli xiaomieliao, xinde juli you chulaile, shuoyi yao buduande xue*)".[93] Along with scientific rationality, another idea back in vogue was the concept of self-reliance (*dulizhizhu, jiligengsheng*).[94] These slogans de-emphasized during Daqing's downfall in the Cultural Revolution were now taken out of the closet and given a new polish.

Art and culture in the form of the sketchbook were now deployed to sew together pieces of memories before and after the Revolution. This artistic enterprise was given greater impact by collating and compiling artistic sketches drawn by artists coming from different communities in China who had resided in Daqing.[95] This carefully-constructed and nationally-derived pictorial representation of the oilfield paralleled a nationwide restoration of the post-Cultural Revolution oilfield. The intent and purpose of the compilation in the foreword revealed that, other than accurate portrayals of workers' expressions, the book served as an educational and propaganda tool (*xuanchuan jiaoyude mude*).[96] Intellectually and culturally, it was a re-instatement of Daqing's relevance to post-Revolution development. Cultural propagation of

---

[92] Renmin Chubanshe, Zhongguo Gongchangdang Zhongyang Weiyuanhui Fuzhuxi Ye Jianying Tongzhi Zai Quanguo Gongye Xuedaqinghuishang De Jianghua (The Speech Given by Vice Chairman Comrade Ye Jianying at the National Chinese Communist Party Central Committee Learn from Daqing Conference) (1977), p. 2. Beijing: Renminchubanshe.

[93] Ibid.

[94] Daqing Wenhua Yishuguan (Daqing Arts and Culture Museum) (1976).

[95] Ibid.

[96] Ibid.

Daqing's revival meant that its validation had gone from latent to manifest approval.

The year 1977 was declared unequivocally as the right time for a revitalized and re-invigorated return to full-speed reconstruction by the industrial and technocratic community. The unmistakable sign of Daqing's restoration in the post-Cultural Revolution period was the re-institution of the National Conference on Learning from Taching in Industry, a conference that enjoyed nationwide attention and Mao's personal praises in the heyday of Daqing fever.[97] The conference was convened at Daqing oilfield on 20 April 1977 and attended by 7,000 delegates nationwide.[98] It marked the triumphant return of Daqing and China's oil modernization and decisively laid to rest any other interpretations of China's top leadership in the future importance of the oilfield. Perhaps, the most meaningful signifier of the reinstatement of the Petroleum Faction was the choice of Vice Premier Yu Qiuli to present the report to the conference.[99]

The opening speech by Hua Guofeng who emerged victorious from the Cultural Revolution struggle as the Chairman of the Central Committee of the Communist Party of China and Premier of the State Council began with the symbolic declaration that Daqing had been reinstated after the "smashing" of the anti-Party Gang of Four (Wang Hungwen, Chang Chun-chiao, Chiang Ching and Yao Wen-yuan).[100] Daqing had become the symbol of the Anti-Gang of Fourisms. Against the backdrop of a celebratory mood, Hua also took the opportunity to legitimize the return of Daqing comrades to their respective units and resume work.[101] The Petroleum Faction technocrats reappeared as quickly as they vanished. In the topsy-turvey world of Chinese politics at this time, the order of appearance was the exact reverse of the intensity of criticism leveled on the technocrats.

Previously, during the Cultural Revolution, the closer the individual was associated with Liu, Deng or even Zhou, the earlier and more

[97] Foreign Languages Press (1977), Publisher's Note.

[98] Ibid.

[99] Ibid.

[100] Ibid., p. 1.

[101] Ibid., p. 2.

severely attacked. But, now, the closer the technocrat was to Zhou or Deng, the faster they got reinstated. Kang Shien reappeared publicly in May 1971 and became the Minister of the Oil and Chemical Industries in January 1975.[102] The rest, mostly vice-ministers, took a little longer. Zhang Zhen resurfaced in September 1974, becoming the vice-minister for the oil and chemical industries in November of the following year.[103] Li Yilin was spotted in public for the first time in September 1974 and became the vice minister for the fuel and chemical industries.[104] Sun Jingwen's reinstatement to vice-minister took a little longer than his contemporaries; he reappeared in public in June 1975 and was identified as the vice-minister for the oil and chemical industries in April 1976.[105] In 1975, the power of the Petroleum Faction was boosted by Yu Qiuli's promotion to Vice-Premier.[106]

As Vice-Premier, Yu was in the public spotlight when he was tasked by the Party Central Committee to present the "important" government report entitled *Mobilizing the Whole Party and the Nation's Working Class and Strive to Build Taching (Daqing)-type Enterprises Throughout the Country* at the National Conference on Learning from Taching (Daqing) in Industry, presided by Mao's short-lived heir-apparent, Chairman Hua Guofeng of the Central Committee of the Chinese Communist Party and Premier of the State Council.[107] The 1977 Conference was described as "a remarkable gathering of unprecedented scale on China's industrial front" and was attended by 7,000 delegates nationwide.[108]

The then supreme leader Chairman Hua instructed delegates of the conference to "take back the spirit of the conference, the Taching (Daqing) experience and the experience of other advanced units, together with the eager expectations of the Party Central Committee

---

[102] Bartke, W. (1977), p. 123.

[103] Ibid.

[104] Ibid., p. 124.

[105] Ibid., p. 125.

[106] Lee, T. H. (1995), pp. 69–70.

[107] Foreign Languages Press (1977), Publisher's Note.

[108] Ibid.

and the people of the whole country for the entire body of workers, cadres and scientific and technical personnel fighting on the industrial front".[109] The fiery words completely authorized Yu's report and other conference materials to be filtered down to post-Cultural Revolution China and reinstate Daqing industrialization as China's goal. Yu also responded quickly to the new order as the new Vice-Premier of the State Council. He attributed the success and smooth running of the conference to "wise leader Chairman Hua".[110]

Yu's bitterness at being persecuted during the Cultural Revolution was revealed in his 1977 speech to 7,000 delegates at the National Conference on Learning from Taching (Daqing) in Industry. He highlighted that "our wise leader Chairman Hua led us in smashing the Wang-Chang-Chiang-Yao 'gang of four' at one blow".[111] He accused the Gang of Four of "repeatedly stirring up the evil wind to oppose Taching (Daqing) and haul down this red banner".[112] He equated the end of the Revolution with the analogy of "the entire industrial front, now freed from the mental shackles imposed by the 'gang of four'"....[113]

Yu also revealed the deep divisions over the Daqing policy during the Cultural Revolution, airing the internal strife over the future of the Chinese oil industry during this period publicly. The position of the Petroleum Faction on the Daqing policy was announced boldly by Yu: "In this Report on the Work of the Government to the Fourth National People's Congress in 1975, Premier Chou (Zhou Enlai) once again called on us to deepen the mass movements — In industry, learn from Taching (Daqing)... The State Council began active preparations to hold a national conference on learning from Taching (Daqing) in industry and the various provinces, municipalities and autonomous regions and departments concerned did much work for this purpose".[114]

---

[109] Ibid., p. 2.

[110] Ibid., p. 42.

[111] Ibid., p. 43.

[112] Ibid., p. 49.

[113] Ibid., p. 45.

[114] Ibid., p. 50.

But their position was savagely attacked by the Gang of Four as Yu revealed: "However, the 'gang of four' tried in every possible way to obstruct and sabotage the convocation of this conference. Chang Chun-chiao shouted: 'It is pointless to learn from Taching (Daqing) at present.' He even told the Gang's followers in Shanghai: 'They go their way, we go ours. Don't give a damn about what they tell you.' The 'gang of four' listed Taching (Daqing) as 'out of bounds' and prohibited comrades in Shanghai from visiting it. When Shanghai workers and staff members went to Taching (Daqing) on a study tour organized by departments under the State Council, the Gang even gave them what they called 'preventive inoculations' before the trip and an 'antidote' after it".[115]

It was no holds-barred as Yu reserved some of the toughest criticisms for Mao's wife but was careful to separate the wife from the Chairman: "The gang, furthermore, opposed Taching (Daqing) and tried to tear down the red banner by attacking the film *Pioneers*, directing the spearhead of their attack at our great leader Chairman Mao and our respected and beloved Premier Chou (Zhou Enlai). Chiang Ching (Jiang Qing) viciously attacked the film as glorifying revisionism and fabricated ten 'charges' against it... Their reactionary arrogance went to the extreme".[116]

Again, the Chairman was insulated from the actions of his wife and the revolution he started: "Chairman Mao promptly wrote a brilliant note on the film, thereby shattering the gang's plot and giving tremendous encouragement to the workers of Taching (Daqing) and the people of the whole country".[117] In Yu's account, even the Chairman's instructions were treated with less reverence than it deserved. Despite Chairman Mao's note to praise the film *Pioneers*, "the 'gang of four', however, did not stop there. They continued to persecute the scenario of *Pioneers* and opposed Chairman Mao's note, obstinately clinging to their counter-revolutionary stand. They tried to consign the film to oblivion, and shelved for 10 years another

[115] Ibid., pp. 50–51.
[116] Ibid., p. 51.
[117] Ibid.

film, *Battle Song of Taching (Daqing)*, made on Premier Chou's instructions".[118]

Yu also condemned the Gang of Four for attacking the field-level staff members in Daqing, including the legendary model worker Ironman Wang. He opened the attack: "Time and again they sent so-called 'fighting groups' to Taching (Daqing) to incite 'overthrowing all,' provoke 'all-round civil war' and ruthlessly persecute Iron Man Comrade Wang Chin-hsi (Wang Jinxi) and a large number of revolutionary cardes and model workers in an attempt to pull down the red banner of Taching (Daqing) at one stroke".[119]

Emphasis was placed on restoring the former glory of Daqing in the ideological realm. Yu ventured: "Chairman Mao pointed out in December 1963: Among the dozens of ministries under the Central Government, there are obviously several which have done better and have a better style of work, for instance, the Ministry of Petroleum Industry. Yet the other ministries simply ignored them, have never bothered to visit them, study their experience and compare notes (highlighted in original text). After this Chairman Mao repeatedly urged us to learn from the Ministry of Petroleum Industry...What the Ministry of Petroleum and Chemical Industries has been able to accomplish is entirely within the reach of all other industrial departments, provided they make energetic efforts".[120]

Chairman Yu's 1977 speech became one of the first large-scale unadulterated public attacks on the Gang of Four and a thinly veiled criticism of the Cultural Revolution. But it also legitimized the restoration of essential activities of the Chinese oil industry. He was the first to advocate the re-opening of "factory-run technical schools and other spare-time technical training institutions which have suspended operation..."[121] during the Cultural Revolution. He wanted enterprises

[118] Ibid., pp. 51-52.
[119] Ibid., pp. 52-53.
[120] Ibid., p. 85.
[121] Ibid., p. 82.

and units to "ensure that workers have adequate time for study".[122] Scientific and technical rationality once again took the front seat as Yu urged Daqing and other "Daqing-type" enterprises to "constantly make new achievements in technical innovations and technical revolution ... and reach the advanced national levels in major technical and economic indices"....[123]

Many figures purged during the Cultural Revolution were given ultimate praise in PRC oil literature and became associated with the industry itself. For example, in a compilation of articles published by the Chinese oil industry press, *Jiannan Chuangye Zhongguo Shiyou Gongye Dierji (The Difficulties of Starting an Industry: The Chinese Oil Industry Series Two)*, Kang Shien intimated that Daqing was indebted to the late premier and was soaked with its blood and sweat (*Daqing Youtian Qintoule Zhou Zhongli de xinxue*) in a piece entitled "*Huainian Jingaide Zhou Enlai Tongzhi (Reminiscing Comrade Zhou Enlai)*".

Kang credited Zhou with "resolutely and wisely protecting the people's oilfield (Daqing) and its staff/unit under complicated and difficult circumstances in 10 tumultuous years of the Cultural Revolution (*Shinian dongluanzhong, Zhouzhongli zai huanjing fuzha eryou jianxiande jingkuangxia, jianding er jizhide baohule zhepian renminde youtian, baohule wei youtian kaifa jianshe zhuochu gongxian de guangda ganbu*)".[124] Zhou was also portrayed by Kang as a selfless leader who worked beyond midnight during his visit to Daqing on 20 June 1962 and rejected repeated pleas for him to take rests earlier than 1 a.m. in the morning.[125]

Similarly, contemporary PRC oil literature praised Deng Xiaoping and Yu Qiuli, crediting the former for having the foresight to propose shifting Chinese oil exploration eastwards as a strategic move and the latter for backing Deng's directions.[126] In the official interpretation

---

[122] Ibid.

[123] Ibid., pp. 87–88.

[124] Kang, S. (1992), p. 2.

[125] Ibid.

[126] ZhangW. (1999), p. 261.

of China's oil industrial history, the *Shiyou Gongye Chubanshe* (China's official oil industry press) cited the eastward shift as being vital for the eventual discovery of Daqing. From these examples (Zhou, Deng and Yu), it can be discerned that both the persecuted and their protectors finally won a long and hard-fought victory in post-Cultural Revolution China.

Chapter

6

Looking Beyond Self-Reliance

From February to June 1976, the Gang of Four (Wang Hongwen, Zhang Chunqiao, and Yao Wen) led by Jiang Qing held several national conferences and interfered with Politburo meetings as well as utilized the media (where their influence was the strongest) to attack the oil export policy and importation of processed materials like Japanese steel.[1] Their targets of attacks were Deng Xiaoping, Yu Qiuli, Kang Shien, Li Xianian and Ye Jianying,[2] all of whom were leaders and allies of the Petroleum Faction.

The Gang of Four accused the Petroleum Faction of the following: "By exporting petroleum, China is shifting the international energy crisis on to the Chinese people and has saved the first and second worlds, i.e., the US, Japan and Western Europe. The State Council is leasing China's natural resources to foreign countries and is engaged in national betrayal. We are importing too many major items, a whole bunch of things at once. The Ministry of Foreign Trade has unrestrainedly imported what China can produce, and limitlessly exported

[1] Lieberthal, K. and Oksenberg, M. (1986), p. 186.

[2] Ibid.

what is badly needed at home. The Ministry has conceded sovereignty over the exploitation of mines and resources to others and tried to run China into the dumping ground, raw material base, repair workshop, and outlet for investment of the imperialist countries."[3]

While high-sounding and moralistic, in fact, Jiang Qing's charge had been proven to be opportunistic because Lieberthal presented evidence that, at an earlier time, Jiang and her allies had professed agreement with the plan to export fuel and raw materials and they also allegedly knew that the plan had the full authorization of Chairman Mao despite the fact that it originated from Zhou Enlai and his Petroleum Faction supporters.[4]

Lieberthal also suggested that it was not the oil exports that were imperiling China's oil supply situation but, instead, shortages in Chinese oil supply had to do with rapid domestic growth, high growth rates in heavy industries, inefficient use of fuel and China's transition from coal to oil-fired thermal power plants as scheduled in the Fourth Five-Year Plan.[5] Jiang had shrewdly used the 1976 energy crisis to her advantage and transitionally stalled the growth of China's economic interactions with Japan. Deliveries to Japan were less than what had been promised with 6.2 MMT of oil delivered in 1976 falling short of the contractually agreed 6.8 MMT; contracts for Japanese and foreign technological importations were controlled in the same year while the Petroleum Faction went out of public view.[6]

During the Cultural Revolution attacks, though the Petroleum Faction went into hiding, they were secretly gathering strength for a counter-attack. Even though the Gang of Four tried to use the self-reliance argument to their advantage by limiting foreign importations and curbing exportation of the oil resource, the Petroleum Faction actually won the technical argument. Daqing at this time had more than enough fuel for China's use, a position that was sustained until

[3] Ibid., pp. 186–187.

[4] Ibid., p. 187.

[5] Ibid.

[6] Ibid.

1993. It was in fact the importation of new technological equipment from Japan and the developed world that would improve China's extraction and use of this resource to help sustain its post-Cultural Revolution re-industrialization. In other words, purchase of foreign equipment was used to boost China's self-reliance in energy, rather than impede it. Foreign equipment helped to increase the quantity of accessible domestic oil resources to prevent China from importing foreign oil while using surplus from such extractions to pay for foreign equipment, recycling profits and preventing Chinese trade deficit.

RECONFIGURATION OF SELF-RELIANCE

However, Chinese insistence on doctrinaire self-reliance for most of its early oil industrial history meant that transformation could not take place bereft of ideological justifications and worldview shifts. Though exports of oil and imports of equipment contradicted the principle of self-reliance, from the Chinese worldview, it is just the opposite. One year later in 1975 after his UN speech on self-reliance, Deng Xiaoping asserted: "In catching up with the industrially advanced countries, the industrially backward countries invariably rely on adoption of the most advanced technology" and China must "learn with open-mindedness all advanced and good things from foreign countries" and "usher in advanced techniques from abroad in a planned and selective manner".[7] The trick was to "export as much as possible" and "aggressively increase production of items that can be exported" to "pay back [for equipment imported]" with the energy products produced.[8] To be self-reliant, in other words, one first had to seek the foreign technologies needed to achieve it in the first place.

Despite virulent attacks by conservatives thereafter, most top Chinese leaders approved this new policy by 1978 with two of the

---

[7] Barnett, D. A. (1981). *China's Economy in Global Perspective*, p. 123. Washington DC: The Brookings Institution.

[8] Ibid.

most important endorsements coming from a postmortem interpretation of Mao's quote published in a 1956 article "On the 10 Major Relationships" when he said: "Our policy is to learn from the strong points of all nations and all countries".[9] The other endorsement came from Mao's successor, Hua Guofeng (Hua Kuo-feng in Wades Giles) who declared that "there should be a big increase in foreign trade".[10]

At the technocratic level, there was also support for Deng's policies with the strongest comments probably coming from the leader of the Petroleum Faction, Yu Qiuli. Yu indicated the need for a bold increase in imports and exports with scientific evaluations and assessments of technologies selected for imports.[11] He laid down a few rules to govern such activities in order to preserve some of the principles behind self-reliance including rejection of imports when such goods can be domestically-produced, allowing imports only when repayment plans are presented by the importing agencies at the same time and emphasis placed on manufacturing equipment instead of finished products.[12]

From a social science perspective, the President of the Chinese Academy of Social Sciences pointed out that "learning advanced things from foreign countries" is actually a condition of self-reliance that needed the combination of the "superiority of the socialist system with the advanced science and technology of the developed capitalist countries."[13] With such interpretations of Deng's statement disseminating to other Chinese elites, Deng Xiaoping had effectively reconciled self-reliance and open door policy in one stroke.

WHY THE SHIFT AWAY FROM SELF-RELIANCE?

This doctrinal reconciliation in fact weakened the PRC's conventional understanding of self-reliance as depending on one's resources bereft of outside help. Many reasons were offered as compulsions for China

---

[9] Ibid., p. 125.

[10] Ibid., p. 126.

[11] Ibid., p. 131.

[12] Ibid.

[13] Lee, T. H. (1995), p. 188.

to veer away from the doctrine of self-reliance towards an open door policy. One of the most important reasons is the acute need to augment China's infrastructure development necessitated by the booming economy in the reform era which was revitalized by the end of the Cultural Revolution as well as the PRC's acceptance of foreign investments. In this aspect, some China historians in the West including Jonathan Spence noted the rudimentary nature of PRC doctrine of oil self-reliance in practice at Daqing. Peasants were described as having been armed with "primitive equipment" and having "only the vaguest sense of the purpose of their efforts".[14] Spence suggested that senior party personnel at the oil fields had "chosen to overemphasize the local people's untrained contributions to the oilfield's development".[15]

US Department of Energy Document DOE/IA-0012 September 1981 agreed with this view, marveling at Chinese oil achievements by late 1961 despite "the use of primitive petroleum exploration and development equipment".[16] It was also baffled by how China was able to achieve its goals 12 months ahead of schedule in its second five-year plan despite the utilization of such equipment and developmental philosophy. Continuing with the observation of Chinese backwardness, the document noted that, in 1975, China's oil industry had "achieved the role of a major producer with equipment and methods regarded as antiquated by the world oil industry".[17]

In addition, while most observers agree that Daqing was a significant success in the Chinese oil industry, not all agree that its exploitation was carried out in the best manner. One of the most notable items of debate is the effectiveness of Soviet-inspired water injection (*zaoqi zhushui*) in developing Daqing. Some in the West criticized the water-injection extraction method as damaging, flooding the oilfield, prematurely aging it in the process. Critiques argued that water extraction in Daqing since its discovery was often implemented without due attention to lateral and vertical changes in reservoir

[14] Spence, J. (1999), p. 563.

[15] Ibid.

[16] US Department of Energy (1981). *Energy Industries Abroad DOE/IA-0012 September 1981*, p. 240. US: Office of International Affairs.

[17] Ibid.

porosity and permeability.[18] Other Western observers, however, disagree with this. For example, Wolfgang Bartke remarked that "the new method of early water flooding adopted by Daqing proved much more efficient than the old methods".[19]

However, water flooding did not always produce the highest quality of oil. Daqing crude was rather heavy and waxy with low gasoline yield during primary distillation.[20] The Central Intelligence Agency (CIA) did a study of Daqing crude properties, summarized in Table 6.1 below, which indicated that gasoline share of Daqing crude was only eight to 8.7 percent of total crude content.[21] The low gasoline content had been readily accepted because there were few private cars in the pre-economic reform era. Diesel and distillate oil that formed

Table 6.1: Characteristics of Daqing crude.

Properties	Daqing Saertu	Lamadian
Specific gravity	0.8615	0.8666
API Gravity	32	
Pour Point (degree Celsius)	32.2-35	
Sulfur (%)	0.06-0.14	
Nitrogen (ppm)	1600	
Wax (%)	22.4	
Distillation yields (%)		
Gasoline (180 degrees Celsius)	8.0	8.7
Light diesel oil (180-350 degrees Celsius)	20.8	18.7
Heavy distillates (350-500 degrees Celsius)	27.1	26.7
Residuum (>500 degrees Celsius)	44.1	43.9

Sources: CIA (1977); Acta Petolei Sinica (1980); Smil, V., *China's Energy* (1976), p. 40. NY: Praeger Publishers.

[18] Hardy, R.W. (1978). *China's Oil Future: A Case of Modest Expectations*, p. 7. Colorado: Westview Press.

[19] Bartke, W. (1977), p. 71.

[20] Smil, V. (1976), p. 39.

[21] Ibid., p. 40.

the bulk of Daqing crude as seen from the Table 6.1 were also much more popular fuels than gasoline.[22]

Other than equipment, Daqing's management techniques were also criticized. Cheng Chu-yuan, a critic of PRC policies, took the mainland authorities to task for devoting "undue attention" to the increase in output of crude oil and neglected prospecting for new fields.[23] In 1983, Cheng was one of the early proponents of Daqing's demise, quoting a CIA analysis that Daqing was already exhausted and that its output had declined from 1982 onwards along with other major Chinese oilfields.[24] Cheng predicted the figure of 90 million tons for 1982, a 15 percent decrease from the year 1979.[25] Updated figures, however, show that Cheng's observation was a little premature and that China's oil production managed to go above the 100 million for some years to come.

On top of depleting output due to outdated technologies and management methodologies, another factor that prompted the PRC to seek foreign input for its oil industry was the acute need to increase production for its own domestic use through the introduction of more energy-efficient technologies. China's oil consumption did increase against a backdrop of stabilizing Daqing output. One reason was China's change in policy which included a shift of industrial emphasis from Soviet-style heavy industrial central planning to light consumer industrial export-driven production.[26] In the pre-reform era, Chinese industrial development followed a Stalinist structure with emphasis on heavy industrial development, coal energy consumption and promotion of small-scale but inefficient industries. Such industries, sheltered from market competition, made China one of the world's most wasteful consumers of fuels.[27] Cheng pointed out that, though by the early 1980s, China used almost the same amount of energy as Japan, the annual Gross

---

[22] Ibid., p. 39.

[23] Cheng, C. (1983). *Mainland China — Why Still Backward?*, p. 35. Taipei: Kuang Lu.

[24] Ibid.

[25] Ibid., p. 36.

[26] Thomson, E. (2001), p. 4.

[27] Smil, V. (1976), p. 5.

National Production (GNP) of the former was only 25 percent of the latter.[28]

Consequently, additional pressures and burdens generated by primitive technologies and management techniques as well as increased Chinese oil consumption and Chinese oil exports required the influx of foreign technologies and management to sustain increased production. Japan became a major contributor in this respect. An increase in Daqing oil production and an encouragement of its export potential were vital for the Chinese leadership to transition Daqing from more than a decade of inward-looking self-reliance and domestication to the formerly taboo topic of capitalistic exports. Moreover, equipment, as well as foreign currency, was badly needed after the Cultural Revolution. Fortunately, Daqing's new aspiration to be an exporter of oil was aided by the powerful backing of a restored Petroleum Faction.

RESTORATION OF PETROLEUM FACTION AND ITS ALLIES

The post-Cultural Revolution reinstatement of the Petroleum Faction allowed their technocratic worldview to remain intact in the Chinese oil industry. This was preserved into the 1980s when Yu Qiuli took over the post of the PLA's General Political Department in 1982, acting as a guarantee for the survival of the Faction through this powerful position.[29] The General Political Department is the most important department within the military in charge of re-assigning military personnel, designating military ranks and managing the retirement system.[30]

Aside from the bureaucracy, in higher political positions were other pro-oil export personalities such as third-tier personality Li Peng who rose from an energy background, second-tier leader Hu Yaobang, a former subordinate of Deng Xiaoping who saw his fortunes rise until his own fall in 1987.[31] At the top echelon of power,

[28] Cheng, C. (1983), p. 38.

[29] Lee, T. H. (1995), p. 66.

[30] Ibid.

[31] Lee, T. H. (1995), p. 56.

paramount leader Deng was favorable towards Chinese oil development. Deng had purged Hua and his supporters from mid-1977 through 1978, replacing 15 out of 20 provincial Party committee first secretaries who were pro-Hua. With this purge, Deng became the undisputed leader of the PRC. The 1980s was, therefore, politically favorable for rapid development of the oil industry.

As the ideological war between the Gang of Four and Hua Guofeng/Zhou Enlai/Deng Xiaoping subsided with advantage towards the latter, Hua reinstated the importance of technocratic planning, technology and industrialization by embracing the recently-deceased Premier Zhou's "four modernization" and revived the "Outline of the 10-Year Plan for the Development of the National Economy (1976–1985)", a plan that called for an influx of foreign capital and industrial technology but mothballed during the Gang of Four era.[32] The PRC invited Japanese business delegations back again with the red carpet treatment, beginning an era of exporting Daqing crude for Japanese technologies.

Many reasons were offered as to why China was compelled to veer away from the doctrine of self-reliance. One of the most important reasons is the acute need to augment China's equipment and infrastructure capabilities — necessitated by the booming economy in the reform era which had been revitalized by the end of the Cultural Revolution as well as the PRC's acceptance of foreign investments. Catching up with the Western scientific and industrial progress in this area was a priority. A ready source of such technical progress was found in Japan.

Deng's economic reforms for China immediately gained the attention of the business sector in Japan. Japan's ambassador to China, Sato Shoji, reported that China was pursuing an ambitious program of modernization and was keen to absorb Western and Japanese technologies for this purpose.[33] PM Fukuda's response was to treat the

---

[32] Lee, C. (1984). *China and Japan: New Economic Diplomacy*, p. 20. California: Stanford University and Hoover Institution Press.

[33] Ogata, S. (1988). *Normalization with China*, p. 87. Berkeley: Institute of East Asian Studies University of California-Berkeley.

Peace and Friendship Treaty with China cautiously and instructed Sato to proceed slowly with the Foreign Ministry in charge of the process.[34] It was only after six years of hard negotiations between both parties following the normalization of Sino-Japanese relations that the Treaty of Peace and Friendship was finally signed on 12 August 1978.

In January 1978, Fujiyama Aiichiro representing the interests of the Japanese business lobby went to China and brought back to Japan China's wish-list of energy, steel and chemicals.[35] A Japanese delegation consisting of members from Idemitsu Kosan, Daikyo Oil, Maruzen Oil, and Kyodo Oil, the syndicate behind International Oil organized to negotiate oil imports from China, arrived in Beijing in January 1973.[36] They were also on a fact-finding mission to evaluate the quality of Chinese crude and determine the price.[37]

A crucial success of this negotiation was the agreement to make Chinese crude oil prices flexible and determinable at the point of importation to reflect higher costs of transportation due to a limited fleet of small Chinese tankers.[38] Following this trip, according to the Asahi Shimbum, 14 leading businessmen initiated an oil import company to handle the Chinese petroleum trade. The newspaper reported that the Chinese had a surplus of oil due to crude oil extraction surpassing its domestic refining capacity and that the Japanese business sector urged China to agree to the supply of one million tons of crude oil.[39]

When the Petroleum faction emerged victorious in the Chinese ideological struggle, Yoshihiro Inayama, President of Nippon Steel made famous by the 1972–1973 "Chinese oil for Japanese steel", also made a spectacular comeback in February 1977[40] to restart the engine on long-term Sino-Japanese relations after the downfall of the conservative Gang of Four. He returned in March 1977 as the head of

[34] Ibid.

[35] Ibid., p. 86.

[36] Wu, Y. (1977). *Japan's Search for Oil*, p. 50. California: Stanford University.

[37] Ling, H.C. (1975), p. 24.

[38] Wu, Y. (1977), p. 50.

[39] Ling, H.C. (1975), p. 24.

[40] Lieberthal, K. and Oksenberg, M. (1986), p. 195.

a Keidranren delegation and met the new post-Mao paramount leader Hua Guofeng where they were able to sign agreements for long-term Chinese exports of oil and other materials in exchange for imports of plants, machinery and steel, setting the target for Chinese oil exports by 1982–1983 at 50 MMT annually.[41]

Inayama was assigned his Chinese counterpart, Vice-Minister of Foreign Trade, Liu Xiwen as a partner to finalize the details of a long-term trade agreement to mobilize associations in both countries to kick-start the momentum on Sino-Japanese trade. The Chinese formed an inter-ministerial committee for this purpose while the Japanese side gathered prominent industrialists, financiers and traders in response.[42] To push for realistic oil diplomacy, both sides decided to do away with the expectation of annual Chinese exports of 50 million tons, taking into consideration Chinese production capacity and domestic Japanese resistance against dependence on Chinese oil.[43]

This post-Cultural Revolution era of outward orientation was perhaps only the second large-scale attempt in the modern history of the Chinese oil industry to institute such a large shift in management direction and philosophy. The first PRC experiment with privatization and outward orientation was, in fact, a cover. The China Oil Trading Company established in the early formative days of the PRC was an outfit entrusted with the task of confiscating foreign-owned stocks in China, particularly from the top three foreign companies in China and compensating them according to standard formulations.[44] Outside these two brief experiments with privatization and export-orientation, only rare and sporadic oil exports took place to North Korea in 1964 and to North Vietnam in 1965 up to 1972.[45] Commentators were unsure if these transactions are of a commercial nature or under

[41] Ibid.

[42] Ibid.

[43] Ibid., p. 196.

[44] Zhongguo Lianyou Gongye (China Oil-Refining Industry) Editorial Team (1989), p. 304.

[45] Park, C. (1975), p. 16.

capacity-building aid.[46] In addition, amounts exported to the Philippines or Thailand in 1974 were considered to be of amounts symbolic of friendship deals rather than substantive commercial value.[47]

INSTITUTIONALIZATION

Sino-Japanese ties were finally formalized with the signing of the LTTA. The first significant element of the LTTA was that it was longer in duration than the 1974 China-Japan Trade Agreement, being eight years in duration.[48] It was also more explicit in its goals, projecting a US$20 billion trade between the two countries in the period between 1978 to 1985 with each side contributing US$10 billion.[49] The fact that such an agreement took such a long time to materialize, even though there were continual overtures to resume relations, was testament to the persistent seduction of economic mutualism in Sino-Japanese relations. The chief items that the Japanese needed from the Chinese during this period were energy commodities, beginning the phase of "(Japanese) technology for (Chinese) oil".

While Japanese energy interests in the LTTA was clear, the Chinese had their own priorities as well. In return for exporting their oil, the Chinese were keen to obtain much-needed foreign currency through this trade and a good vantage point to begin re-industrialization after the Cultural Revolution. Daqing's slow post-Cultural Revolution increase in oil output was attributed to a lack of capital and heavy industrial machinery output.[50] Other than hoping for an increase in output, capital and technologies were also needed for sustainable exploitation.[51] In this sense, the crucial sweetener for persuading the Chinese to sign the agreement was a US$7–8 billion transfer of

[46] Ibid., p. 48.

[47] Ibid.

[48] Newby, L. (1988), p. 7.

[49] Ibid.

[50] Horsnell, P. (1997), p. 47.

[51] Ibid., p. 50.

Japanese technologies and US$2–3 billion worth of heavy machinery and construction materials to China.[52] Recognizing China's economic situation, the LTTA agreed to China's deferred payments for these goods, an economic carrot that would replay over and over again.[53] The next chapter will study China's shift from self-reliance to reliance on Japan in detail.

---

[52] Newby, L. (1988), p. 7.

[53] Ibid.

Chapter

7

Reliance on Japan

OIL CRISIS

Before the onset of the 1973 oil crisis, Japan's Ministry of Foreign Affairs held a cautious attitude in assessing China's oil resources. It was torn between two views. One view proclaimed China to be oil-deficient based on three pieces of evidence. First, China's geological makeup was said to be mostly older than oil-bearing stratum, complex in make-up and stratification, non-conducive to oil potential.[1] Second, China's long ancient history of landscaping by men has resulted in the oilfields being obscured by mountain ranges influenced by such activities.[2] Third, the laws regulating the distribution of oil are ungoverned by well-established rules and there are few oilfields other than the ones discovered accidentally in China.[3]

According to Japan's Ministry of Foreign Affairs, younger geologists and oil experts took an opposite view and did not discount the

[1] Gaimusho Keizaikyoku Keizaitogoka (Japan's Ministry of Foreign Affairs Economics Bureau Economics Statistics Section) (1970), p. 162.

[2] Ibid., p. 163.

[3] Ibid., p. 162.

possibility of China having rich deposits of oil. First, it is postulated that, since China's peripheral lands like Burma and Kuriles which are similar in make-up have oil deposits, it is expected that China being located in the center of these oil-bearing places would also have oil deposits too.[4] Second, despite China's many mountain ridges and the possibility of oil deposits disrupted by ancient landscaping by men, conditions are still favorable towards the prevalence of oil-bearing basins.[5] The prospect of Chinese oil became increasingly important by the day because Japanese oil consumption had increased 137 times over from 32,000 to 4.4 million barrels per day from 1948 to 1972.[6] This increase was also attributed to the growth in Japan's automobile industry with the car industry producing 4.1 million vehicles in 1968, up from 69,000 in 1955, with 85 percent of the cars used within the domestic market.[7]

Unexpectedly, an external event intervened to push Japan closer to China in 1973 and basically put an end to this debate. Japan's greatest postwar economic crisis came with the shock created by the oil embargo of the Organization of Petroleum Exporting Countries (OPEC). OPEC classified Japan along with other Western countries like West Germany and Italy as "unfriendly nations", causing anxieties within Japan that they might not be able to secure a steady supply of oil.[8]

According to the Japanese government's statistics from the Enerugicho (energy agency), in 1956 the Japanese economy was still mainly coal-powered with coal constituting 49.7 percent of the country's energy needs and oil in the second place at 21.9 percent.[9] But in

---

[4] Ibid., p. 162–163.

[5] Ibid., p. 163.

[6] Yergin, D. (1991). *The Prize: The Epic Quest for Oil, Money and Power*, p. 541. NY: Simon and Schuster.

[7] Ibid., p. 546.

[8] Shinichi, K. (Diplomacy and the Military in Showa Japan). In *Showa The Japan of Hirohito*, Gluck, C. and Graubard, S. R. (eds.), pp. 170–171. New York and London: WW Norton and Company.

[9] Takashi, K. *Shigen Enerugicho* (*Japan's Department of Energy and Resources*), p. 15. Japan: Kyouikukai Gyousei Series 15, Japan Administrative Series 15.

1965, a decade later, the figures basically reversed and, by 1971 near the oil crisis, Japan's dependence on oil for its energy sources had grown to 73.6 percent while coal shrank to 17.5 percent.[10]

Oil-deficient Japan was suddenly hit by soaring inflation, a dampener on export growth. Japan's Gross National Product (GNP) which registered at an annual rate of 9.44 percent between 1955 and 1973 suddenly plummeted to 0.3 percent in 1974.[11] The panic that ensued created a shortage in daily necessities and record high prices that made life unbearable for the Japanese. Japan now had a real incentive to trade with China, especially targeted at its oil reserves. Aside from economic imperatives, in terms of foreign policy, the oil crisis also made the Japanese realize for the first time in its postwar history that it had to make certain decisions in international relations commensurate with its national and industrial strength after its postwar recovery.[12]

EARLY CONTACTS

With growing realization of problems in the economy on the Chinese side and careful appeasement of Washington on the Japanese side, small steps were taken to create some semblance of economic relations prior to the official resumption of ties between the two countries. Stopgap Sino-Japanese trade and commercial interactions was guided by a Liao-Takasaki Memorandum of 1962 which amongst its stipulations included a provision for annual review of this economic relationship. The Memorandum was forged between Premier Zhou Enlai and Matsumura Kenzo with the blessings of Prime Minister Ikeda Hayato and subsequently became known as the Liao-Takasaki agreement named after the two signatories of the treaty, Liao Cheng-chih (deputy chief of the Chinese Staff Office of Foreign Affairs) and Takasaki Tatsunosuki (wartime vice-president of the Manchurian Heavy Industries Company and former director of the Economic

[10] Ibid.

[11] Garon, S. (1997). *Molding Japanese Minds*, p. 173. New Jersey: Princeton.

[12] Shinichi, K. (1992). p. 172.

Planning Agency).[13] The Liao-Takasaki agreement envisioned a bilateral import-export trade to the tune of US$180 million and facilitated the establishment of permanent trade offices in the capitals of both countries.[14]

When the US restored ties with the Chinese in 1972, it freed the Japanese of the need to have economic exchanges with the Chinese in a clandestine manner. According to Yuan-li Wu's publication, *Japan's Search for Oil* which is a case study on economic nationalism and international security, Japan was eager to ride on "...the ploy of Nixon and Kissinger in 1971–1972 in exploiting the mutual hostility and suspicion between Moscow and Peking to its own advantage..." and "...the possibility of approaching China on oil became an attractive reality...".[15] In 1972, the Japanese declared that the peace treaty signed with the Nationalist government in Taiwan would be invalid while the Chinese government promised to abandon requests for war reparations from the Japanese government.[16] These initiatives paved the way for what would eventually be energy diplomacy between the two states with the Japanese buying Chinese petroleum and extending long-term credits for Chinese industrial plant projects.

To reap economic benefits and to satisfy the supporters of resumption of Sino-Japanese diplomatic ties on both sides, the post-war construction of a neutral space was initiated. To achieve this, forces in both countries formulated the separation of politics from economics. Economic rationality was seen to be neutral and could be used freely to defeat political opponents of resumption of ties between the two East Asian neighbors. The concept of separation of politics and economics emphasized the real and imagined constructs of China's boundless energy potential, large energy consumer market and Japan's complementary economic position as

[13] Sadako, O. (1988), p. 12.

[14] Ibid.

[15] Wu, Y. (1977), p. 38.

[16] Iriye, A. (1992). *China and Japan in the Global Setting*, p. 124. Cambridge: Harvard University Press.

a trading partner and supplier of technologies and management knowhow.

Domestically, Japanese technocrats and political factions in favor of energy ties with China accentuated Japan's domestic weakness in energy sources and highlighted the potential of China's energy fields. Backed by strong political forces supporting continuity in the relations with China, the construct of a boundless resource market for Japanese industrialization was coupled with its image as a possible source of salvation for Japan's growing energy needs and postwar recovery and continued growth.

THE INFORMATION-GATHERING PHASE

The subtle contacts that Japan had with China in the postwar years were useful in maintaining continuity that could easily be tapped for oil exchanges. Japan soon became privy to formerly confidential oil data. For example, when Japan eyed Chinese oil resources as a possible supplement to its foreign oil imports during the years on the oil crisis in the 1970s, nobody really knew the real state of the Chinese oil industry or its crucial statistics and numbers. The PRC had imposed a blackout on oil data in 1960 and the real major source of information about Chinese oil industry came from a Chinese defector from the Ministry of Petroleum Industry who fled to Taiwan with a significant amount of confidential data.[17]

As China got re-engaged on the international stage, they chose to reveal this privileged information only to two preferred sources. The first individual privy to such knowledge was American journalist Edgar Snow and the other was the visiting Japanese Foreign Minister Masayoshi Ohira in early 1974. Both obtained this privileged information directly from the horse's mouth — Premier Zhou Enlai.[18] Zhou told Snow that China's oil production was 20 million tons and

[17] Cheng, C. (1976), p. 85.

[18] Ibid., p. 18.

revealed to the Japanese Foreign Minister that China's oil production was 50 million tons for 1973.[19]

In 1974, permission was also granted to Ryutaro Hasegawa, Chairman of the Japan-China Oil Import Council, to visit China on an information-gathering mission. Hasegawa was granted an audience with Chinese officials and given a personal tour of Chinese oilfields.[20] He returned to Japan and organized an airport press conference in which he released some statistics and projections that provided some of the world's first glimpses into some of the world's most secretive oilfields.[21] Subtle postwar continuity in contact despite Washington disapproval had its privileges after all. Hasegawa announced in August 1974 that the Japan-China Oil Import Council members which included a number of oil companies and trading firms would import 350,000 tons of Chinese oil during the third quarter of 1974 and that the total oil import from China in 1975 would be sharply higher: three to four million tons in the first half of the year and 10 million tons in the second half.[22]

Though the revelation of information seemed unimportant, this gesture was one of the most closely-watched events among China watchers at that time. The frustrating lack of data and information about the Chinese oil industry was cited by many first-generation US observers of the postwar Chinese oil industry. Japan was no exception. In fact, recorded within the *Chugoku Tariku no Shigen to Chukyo no Shigen Seisaku (Mainland China's Resources and Chinese Communist Party's Resource Policies*) report published by Japan's Ministry of Foreign Affairs, the lack of information about the Chinese Communist Party's (CCP) oil policies was cited as a matter of "grave concern" (*jyuudaina kanshin*) to Japan.[23] Up till Zhou's revelation to Ohira and Hasegawa's visit, the free world knew very little about Daqing or its exact locations. The release

---

[19] Bartke, W. (1977), pp. 22–23.

[20] Cheng, C. (1976), p. 37.

[21] Ibid., p. 37.

[22] Wu, Y. (1977), p. 51.

[23] Gaimusho Keizaikyoku Keizaitogoka (Japan's Ministry of Foreign Affairs Economics Bureau Economics Statistics Section) (1970), introduction.

of information paved the way for Sino-Japanese oil relations to open up dramatically.

EARLY OIL TRADE CONTACT (1972)

With Japanese observance of the Zhou principles and US normalization of relations with China in 1972, trade between Japan and China progressed steadily with the Chinese increasing their oil exports from 29 to 45 tons between 1972 to 1974.[24] Japan was attracted by the shorter distance to Daqing's low-sulfur Chinese oil as opposed to other non-Middle Eastern sources in Southeast Asia.[25] Feelers were sent out from the Chinese side in 1972 to indicate that they were interested in increasing oil exports to Japan.[26] The February 1972 Shanghai Communique and September 1972 formal establishment of diplomatic relations with Japan allowed Chinese petroleum bureaucrats to broaden contacts with the Japanese and to travel more widely. Zhang Wenbin, one of the most senior petroleum officials at the time, was part of a prestigious 10-member Chinese economic mission to Japan in March 1972.[27]

In May 1973, Ch'ien Jen-yuan (Qian Renyuan), the prominent Chinese authority on high polymer, led a delegation of six technical experts on a visit to Japan.[28] Then the exchanges got elevated to a higher level. In 1973, the Japanese Minister of International Trade and industry (MITI) Yasuhiro Nakasone visited Beijing to discuss trade involving raw materials for China's items of interests from Japan.[29] When Nakasone met Zhou Enlai in 1973, Zhou offered one million metric tons of petroleum for trade with Japan.[30] Zhou also

---

[24] Rothenberg, M. (1977). *Whither China: The View From the Kremlin*, p. 123. Washington DC: Center for Advanced International Studies University of Miami.

[25] Wu, Y. (1977), p. 50.

[26] Lieberthal, K. and Oksenberg, M. (1986), p. 180.

[27] Ibid., p. 179.

[28] Cheng, C. (1976), p. 141.

[29] Lieberthal, K. and Oksenberg, M. (1986), p. 180.

[30] Ibid.

separately told Japan's Foreign Minister Ohira in 1973 that China's 1973 oil output (predominantly Daqing's) was 50 million tons.[31] This revelation sent shockwaves through Japan, especially among international observers who had been underestimating China's oil potential.[32] Initial proposed amounts in this trade was one million tons of Chinese oil in 1973 with another three million tons planned in 1974.[33]

Other than the state, Japanese oil conglomerates often working in tandem with the government sent a four-member delegation of company representatives to Beijing to evaluate the quality of Chinese oil and to negotiate the prices. This trip was first reported in the *Mainichi Shimbum*, a leading Japanese business daily.[34] After this fact-finding mission, *Asahi Shimbum* then followed up with an article stating that 14 leading business executives would collectively handle the importation of oil into Japan.[35]

MITI promptly organized a Japanese consortium to sign a contract in April 1973 confirming this and the first tanker of Chinese oil arrived in Japan in September of that year. In 1973, China forwarded the first numerically significant shipment (one million metric tons) of high-quality low sulfur content oil to Japan,[36] arriving at the Idemitsu Hyogo refinery on 21 May 1973.[37] The sale of this one million tons of Daqing crude generated US$32.6 million for the Chinese state.[38] In September 1973, the Vice-President of International Oil and board chairperson of the Kansai head office of the International Trade Association announced that a 600 km pipeline from Daqing to Chin-chou would be completed by end 1974.[39]

---

[31] US Government Printing Office (1974), p. 43.

[32] Woodard, K. (1980), p. 127.

[33] US Government Printing Office (1974), p. 45.

[34] Ling, H. C. (1975), p. 24.

[35] Ibid.

[36] Ibid., p. 43. Wu Yuan-li listed the first shipment as amounting to 13,000 kiloliters (Wu, Y. (1977), p. 50).

[37] Wu, Y. (1977), p. 50.

[38] Cheng, C. (1976), p. 158.

[39] Wu, Y. (1977), p. 50.

In another development in June 1974, the Vice-President of the Japanese International Oil Trading Company announced that China agreed to supply Japan with four million tons of oil in 1974 with 2.5 million tons coming from Daqing.[40] By August 1974, the Japanese informed Beijing that they were interested in procuring an annual intake of 30 million tons of crude oil from China and offered cooperation in the aspect of loading capacities in the ports of shipment and the supply of tankers.[41] In October 1974, the Chinese responded to the Japanese request and reduced their price to US$12.80 per barrel and promised Japan to supply her with crude oil to the extent of eight million tons in 1975.[42] The eventual 1974 volume agreed upon was four million tons, of which three million were imported through the International Oil Trading Company (Kokusai Sekiyu) and one million through the Japan-China Oil Import Company.[43] The four million tons of Chinese crude eventually shipped to Japan came mainly from Daqing.[44]

BENEFITING FROM JAPAN'S HELP

Japan was, in many ways, linked to the success of Daqing. It supplied steel pipes for Daqing's pipelines. Japan was also the source of information for the rest of the world on Daqing, helping to publicize its export potential just as China was opening up. The jewel in the crown was Japan's new role as Daqing crude's largest customer. Bilateral trade increased two times between 1972 to 1973 and tripled in the next five years with Japan holding on to its leading position in the Chinese markets.[45] The 1973 oil cartel embargo following the Arab-Israeli conflicts became a powerful impetus for Sino-Japanese oil trade. Under the Zhou principles

---

[40] Bartke, W. (1977), p. 40.

[41] Ibid.

[42] Ibid.

[43] Ibid., p. 41.

[44] Cheng, C. (1976), p. 158.

[45] Iriye, A. (1992), p. 127.

of 1970[46] and with the US normalization of relations with China in 1972, trade between Japan and China progressed steadily with the Chinese increasing their oil exports from 29 to 45 tons between 1972 to 1974.[47]

Sino-Japanese oil trade was two-way in nature with Tokyo buying Chinese oil and Beijing buying Japanese equipment. For example, Chinese government officials and the Nippon Kokan Company (Japan's leader in pipeline) negotiated for the sale of onshore oil pipelines 60 cm in diameter as part of the 715 mile pipeline connecting Daqing and Chinwangtao.[48] Japanese export credits granted in 1973 with an annual interest rate of 6 percent and a repayment period of about five years greatly enlarged China's ability to import, resulting in a flurry of large-scale contracts for integrated plants in 1973.[49]

One of the most crucial items that China imported from Japan during this period was steel pipes to make oil pipelines. Contracts were sometimes specifically designed for Chinese needs, e.g. Japan Steel Tube was requested by the Chinese to be the PRC's consultant in selecting oil pipes that were suitable for transporting Daqing's low sulfur and high-viscosity oil, techniques for heating stations and offshore oil pipelines.[50] From 1968 to 1975, the PRC imported 328,000 tons of steel pipes from Japan, almost equivalent to the amount that China itself produced.[51]

The reason for the importation despite domestic production was because Chinese-made steel was not able to withstand high pressures in large pipes unlike the technologically more advanced pipes from Japan.[52] Because of this crucial item from Japan, China was able to

[46] The "Zhou principles" included stipulations that Japanese companies trading with China had to mandatorily declare that they were not affiliated with US companies as joint-ventures or subsidiaries, were not engaged in trade with Taiwan or South Korea, and withheld from arms supplies to US forces in Vietnam.

[47] Rothenberg, M. (1977), p. 123.

[48] Cheng, C. (1976), p. 133.

[49] Ibid., p. 144.

[50] Wu, Y. (1977), p. 50.

[51] Barnett, D. A. (1981), p. 446.

[52] Ibid.

construct close to 3,500 km of pipeline with 2,000 km more under construction by 1976 with diameters from 20 to 61 cm,[53] with the bigger ones likely to be from Japan. Other estimates are between eight to 24 inches with the latter dimensions imported from Japan.[54] Some of these imported steel pipes from Japan must have been critical for China's achievement in constructing Daqing's 1,152 km pipeline to Qinhuangdao (Chinhuangtao). When it was completed in 1974, the pipeline crossed rivers at 260 points of its length, railways at 40 points and highways at 200 points and pumping stations were set up at every 60–70 km.[55]

Japanese demand for Chinese oil fuelled infrastructure construction and modernization in the PRC with two major pipelines (Daqing-Qinhuangdao and Daqing-Dalian) servicing the oil export trade to Japan.[56] Japan readily advanced loans to search for new oilfields in China, especially in the Daqing area.[57] A pipeline was also scheduled for construction from Daqing to Dalian (Dairen in Japanese) to pump three to four million metric tons of crude oil for export to Japan in 1974.[58]

LEARNING FROM JAPAN

From the Japanese perspective, some Japanese viewed Chinese oil exports at a time of oil crisis as "*koui* or kind intentions"[59] and also extended a cooperative spirit in return. Japan also began to visualize herself as a better disseminator of modernity to China. Proponents of this culturally-specific argument pointed out that, since Japan is a "daughter of Chinese civilization", she was able to understand China's cultural sensitivities better, making her a natural fit for investing in China.[60]

---

[53] Ibid.

[54] Hardy, R.W. (1978), p. 15.

[55] Bartke, W. (1977), p. 33.

[56] Woodard, K. (1980), p. 139.

[57] Newby, L. (1988), p. 21.

[58] Ling, H. C. (1975), p. 2.

[59] Tatsu, K. (2002), p. 32.

[60] Reichauer, E. O. (1970). *Japan: The History of a Nation*. New York: Alfred A. Knopf and Newby, L. (1988), p. 45.

Foreign observers also noted this phase of strong Sino-Japanese oil collaboration. Vaclav Smil dubbed this period of interaction and learning from Japan as a period of studying "China's great Asian example"[61] as the China aspired to learn from Japan's highly-acclaimed efficient energy consumption. China sent about 250 scientific and technical delegations (totally 1,100 representatives) to Japan in 1981 alone and, between 1979 and 1982, 960 Chinese students entered Japanese universities and other research institutes.[62] In return, the Chinese welcomed 480 Japanese students into their tertiary education system.[63] At the official level, between 1972 to 1980, at least half of the 80 foreign delegations visiting China were Japanese and at least seven major energy delegations were sent by the PRC to Japan between 1972 to 1976[64] with specialized energy trade and technology personnel involved from both sides.[65]

According to Kim Woodard, hundreds of Japanese technical personnel have been stationed at or have visited various Chinese energy industry construction projects from Sino-Japanese rapprochement up till 1980, and 40 percent of Japanese energy delegations were specialized in some aspect of the refining and petrochemical industries while another 30 percent were managing China's oil exports to Japan.[66] Some analysts went as far as to comment that, during this era of exchanges, the Chinese leadership "felt confident in relying on Japan, rather than on the United States, as the major source of its imported capital products and technology".[67]

Western observers like Randall Hardy saw Sino-Japanese oil interactions as an economic as much as diplomatic bond. Hardy touted Chinese oil as the "single most important trading commodity between

---

[61] Smil, V. (1990), p. 96.

[62] Lee, C. (1984), pp. 140–141.

[63] Ibid., p. 141.

[64] Woodard, K. (1980), p.137.

[65] Ibid., p. 138.

[66] Ibid.

[67] Zhang, D. D. (1997). *Transformation in the Political Economy of China's Relations with Japan in the Reform Era Pacific Economic Papers No. 265*, p. 3. Canberra: Australia-Japan Research Centre.

the two countries" as Chinese oil exports to Japan rose from 20,000 bpd in 1973 to 160,000 bpd in 1975 and priced from US$3.75 per pre-oil crisis barrel to US$14.80 per oil crisis barrel in early 1974.[68] According to Gu Rubai of the Bank of China and Yukinori Ito of the Export-Import Bank of Japan, total Japanese energy loans to China between 1979 to 1993 totaled US$9.4 billion.[69]

Sometimes, the affinity between China and Japan were so pronounced that both sides discovered that they had some similar systems installed. For example, when a Deputy bureau head of the Chinese petroleum industry, Guan Zhenyuan, visited Japan in 1982 to study Japanese management techniques, one of his stops was Sony where the Japanese hosts introduced the management technique of having 10-minute consultation and updating sessions before embarking on the project work.[70] Guan later remarked that, in fact, a similar system had been installed at Daqing for 20 years prior to 1982.[71] Such observations hinted at the compatibility in some areas of managements systems between China and Japan.

In this period of collaborating with and learning from Japan, Chinese representatives from the State Geological Bureau (SGB), the Ministry of Petroleum Industry, the Petroleum Company of China and the China National Oil and Gas Exploration and Development Corporation (CNOGEDC) hosted the Japan National Oil Development Corporation (JNODC) for nearly an unprecedented one month starting from June 1978, perhaps the longest ever the Chinese industry had done so since the departure of the Soviet advisor.

The delegation from the JNODC which was a government-funded public agency in foreign oil exploration and development supported by Japanese trade associations like Keidanren and Keizai Doyukai was equally stellar in membership. Its thirteen-member delegation led by the JNODC Vice-President Miyazaki Jin and Director

---

68 Hardy, R.W. (1978), p. 60.

69 Paik, K. W. (1995). *Gas and Oil in Northeast Asia*, p. 30. Great Britain: The Royal Institute of International Affairs.

70 Chen, D. K. (1994), p. 281.

71 Ibid.

Matsuzawa Akira consisted of experts in the field of geophysical prospecting, geology, geochemistry, drilling, facilities, production, refining, finance and law.[72] The JNODC also enjoyed the support of Inayama, the broker of the LTTA, and his organization, Japan China Economic Association (JCEA).[73] The JNODC delegation was taken to Daqing, China's leading petroleum and geological institutes as well as a never seen before newly drilled oilfield in Bohai.[74] This was a tremendous amount of openness on the part of the Chinese, allowing the Japanese to be exposed to and acquire a wealth of data about the Chinese oil industry.

In return, the Japanese extended the first six postwar yen loans to the PRC worth up to 50 billion yen in the fiscal year 1979 to fund six Chinese developmental projects. Two of them were intimately linked to Daqing. The first was an expansion of Beijing-Qinhuangdao (Jing-Qin) railway line to ease existing congestion as well as replace lines declining in condition. A new double-track railway line (127 km) was added while the existing line (150 km) was upgraded into a double-tracked line, costing US$650 million.[75]

Qinhuangdao in Hebei which was linked to Daqing by pipeline and used to export crude oil to Japan was expanded with a new deep water, ice-free wharf added costing US$160 million.[76] Japan's loans were crucial in this area because, up till then, China did not have adequate port facilities with the largest in Dalian accommodating only 100,000 dead weight tons (dwt) and Qinhuangdao able to handle only 50,000 dwt.[77] Tankers classed at 50,000 dwt were mostly of 1950s technology.[78] Japan's help in this area enabled China to work towards achieving the coveted 200,000 plus dwt status in order to accommodate supertankers to export its oil overseas.[79] This would bring China

[72] Lee, C. (1984), p. 79.

[73] Ibid.

[74] Ibid.

[75] Ibid., p. 125.

[76] Ibid.

[77] Hardy, R. W. (1978), pp. 14–15.

[78] Akira, O. (1986). *Sekiyu* (*Oil*), p. 183. Japan: Nihon Keizai Hyouronsha.

[79] Hardy, R. W. (1978), p. 14.

back on par with late 1960s and early 1970s standard with potential for greater expansion.[80]

CHALLENGES — JAPANESE DOMESTIC CONSUMPTION

However, Sino-Japanese cooperation over Daqing had its fair share of problems — both economic and political. Domestically, there was also a shift in Japanese domestic priorities. Cracks in the LTTA deal began to show from the second half of the 1970s to the 1980s. One of the major issues was the dip in Japanese oil demand. This occurred as early as 1975 when oil prices began to demonstrate a downward trend,[81] creating pressures from the Japanese side to request for lower oil prices when trading with the Chinese under the LTTA. Japan's own national campaign to get its population to cut down on the consumption of oil was also unexpectedly successful. Following the oil shock, savings campaigns, social education and New Life austerity campaigns came together with such ferocity that it immediately reminded the Japanese of the wartime years.[82] The first sign of troubles for Sino-Japanese oil interactions came when Japanese oil importation from China declined in 1976 and 1977 after two years of strong growth in this bilateral trade.[83]

IRRATIONAL EXUBERANCE

From the early phase of the relationship, Japan quickly advanced loans to search for new oilfields in China, especially in the Daqing area.[84] There was a feeling that, if Daqing could be discovered so easily with relative ease and basic technologies, capital infusion and more advanced equipment (including those originating from Japan) might give rise to more discoveries of oilfields.[85] This was perhaps

---

[80] Akira, O. (1986), p. 183.

[81] Lieberthal, K. and Oksenberg, M. (1986), p. 184.

[82] Garon, S. (1997). *Molding Japanese Minds*, p. 173. New Jersey: Princeton.

[83] Hardy, R.W. (1978), p. 18.

[84] Newby, L. (1988), p. 21.

[85] Horsnell, P. (1997), pp. 47–48.

a period of irrational exuberance as figures were cranked up on the Japanese side in expectation of a bountiful oil harvest from China. According to Woodard, some of these exaggerated figures also came from the Chinese who managed to convince some Japanese experts that 100 tons of Chinese oil might be available for export to Japan by 1980.[86] Some Japanese importers believed then that China's production would reach 70 millions tons in 1974 and 100 million tons in 1976,[87] (the actual figures achieved were 64.850 and 87.156 respectively). Others, even expected 400 million tons in 1980[88] while the actual figure was in fact 105.941.

One popular explanation for the over-optimistic assessment of Chinese oil potential was the argument that China was keen to lure Japan away from strategically aligning with the Soviet Union through the oil trade.

BALANCE OF POWER VIS-À-VIS THE SOVIET UNION

Outside the economic mutualism, Sino-Japanese oil trade was also a form of strategic alliance targeted at the Soviet Union and even Washington in a subtle manner. The PRC felt threatened by the 1969 Sino-Soviet border clashes that brought ideological conflict into the open in which China was confronted by one of the world's only two superpowers at the site of one of the world's longest borders in the world. A sense of urgency in mutualism was strengthened in 1968 when both the EC and the PRC were unnerved by Soviet intervention in Czechoslovakia and the unfurling of the 1968 Brezhnev doctrine whereby the Soviet Union reserved the right to intervene in any socialist countries in the Soviet bloc.

China did not want Japan to sway to the side of the Soviets by becoming dependent on Russian oil. By using greatly increased promises of oil for Japan, China managed to persuade her from signing a treaty with the USSR for imports of Russian oil from the Yellow Sea

[86] Woodard, K. (1980), p. 127.

[87] Park, C. (1975), p. 23.

[88] Ibid., p. 24.

through a pipeline or a Siberian oil deal.[89] In 1973, when the Japanese trade federation Keidanren visited China, the latter pledged to export 10 percent of Chinese oil production (40 million tons a year) by 1980 if the Japanese refrain from collaborating with the Soviets in the Tjumen pipeline project.[90]

When Yoshihiro Inayama agreed to buy 15 million tons of oil by 1981, the Chinese reportedly was willing to sell up to 50 tons of Chinese crude in order to pull Japan closer to China away from the Soviets.[91] Sino-Japanese cooperation in oil did an about-turn on Japan's previous foreign policy of neutrality characterized as "ominidirectional" and "equidistance"[92] from the Soviet Union and China. The Chinese oil charm offensive together with the convergence of other issues, including Soviet refusal to link Soviet-Japan oil trade with concessions on the Northern Territories,[93] scuttled Soviet-Japan cooperation in favor of the PRC.

The PRC managed to persuade the Japanese of the ease in which Chinese oil could be tapped using existing pipelines and oilfields already in operation without the need for additional investments in comparison with Soviet oil which still required capital for its development.[94] The Chinese offer was available as long as Tokyo restrained its industry and private sector/finance from touching the Siberian oil projects.[95] China also sold oil to Japan at prices below market rate in order to lure Japanese investments to China and forgo Siberian energy development projects.[96] The Chinese hoped to counter Soviet Siberian quantities of oil deposits by accelerating deliveries of their own much smaller oil reserves. Daqing made this possible. In addition, the Central Intelligence Agency (CIA) believed

[89] Bartke, W. (1977), pp. 39 and 56.

[90] Woodard, K. (1980), p. 127.

[91] Jain, R. K. (1977). *China and Japan 1949-1976*, p. 122. India: Humanities Press of New Jersey.

[92] Keith, R. C. (1986), p. 29.

[93] Ibid., p. 27.

[94] Woodard, K. (1980), p. 126.

[95] Ibid.

[96] Downs, E. S. (2000), p. 43.

that the Chinese inflated their projected figures for 1980 exports in order to lure the Japanese away from the Siberian option.[97]

TRANSFORMATION IN SINO-JAPANESE OIL INTERACTIONS

China also became infected with a problem that plagued almost all of Japan's trading partners. They were concerned with a widening deficit in the trade with Japan in 1975 which came up to US$728 million as compared to US$118 million in 1972.[98] *Keidanren* (leading semi-official Japanese trade organization) representatives led by its president, Doko Toshio, went to China in October 1975 to urge the Chinese to raise oil exports to Japan as a solution.[99] Oil was used to temporarily defuse the economic tensions. One month later, Japan's Minister of International Trade and Industry Komoto Toshio and Chinese Vice-Premier Li Xiannian both agreed to continue with a stable oil supply.[100] Japan then came up with a five-year plan to systematize oil imports from China, agreed to purchase 10 million metric tons of Daqing crude in 1977 and to increase the figure to 15 million metric tons by 1982.[101]

By 1978, while bilateral trade of both countries rose to US$5 billion, China's trade deficit with Japan hit the US$1 billion mark, a result of trading low-value added primary raw materials with higher-value added technological goods. This added to overheated rapid Chinese economic development which resulted in the Chinese side canceling Japanese contracts (worth US$2.6 billion) to cool down growth to a realistic level.[102] In response to this cooling of economic trade ties, the Japanese government released US$2 billion worth of loans (Bank of China and the Export-Import Bank of Japan were signatories)

[97] Hardy, R.W. (1978), p. 3.
[98] Lee, C. (1984), p. 17.
[99] Ibid.
[100] Ibid.
[101] Ibid.
[102] Newby, L. (1988), p. 11.

to the Chinese to nudge them to revive economic cooperation once again.[103]

DIFFERING EXPECTATIONS

On the supply side, heady exuberance in the 1970s missed the fact that the Chinese petroleum industry had been severely sabotaged by the disastrous Cultural Revolution and, in addition, because of the chaos, many new Chinese oilfields were unworked on.[104] With the signing of the LTTA, oil export from China suddenly surged 12–13 percent.[105] New oilfields had to be located quickly to meet this sudden increase in oil demand. The pressures for new sources of oil to meet both domestic requirements as well as sudden increases in Japanese market demand undoubtedly created some tensions between the two countries. Moreover, many of the oilfield surveys funded by easily obtainable Japanese loans proved to be unusable.[106]

Soviet press labeled Chinese setbacks in the late 1970s as the "end of the Chinese oil bluff".[107] Ronald C Keith even argued along the lines of a conspiracy theory that the Petroleum Faction might have deliberately encouraged wildly positive speculations of Chinese oil potential in order to capitalize on high oil prices as a convenient solution for Chinese purchases of foreign, including Japanese, technologies in the process of rapid modernization.[108] Kim Woodard highlighted the strategic dimensions of Chinese motivations in drawing Japanese oil interest away from the USSR as Japanese purchases of Russian oil would have seen the construction of trans-Siberian pipelines or railroad along the Sino-Russo border giving the Soviet Union improved access to the border and supply routes for their troops.[109]

---

[103] Ibid., p. 40.
[104] Ibid., p. 21.
[105] Ibid.
[106] Ibid., p. 22.
[107] Keith, R. C. (1986), p. 8.
[108] Ibid., p. 6.
[109] Woodard, K. (1980), p. 7.

Smil, a longtime critique of Chinese and foreign claims of the emergence of China as an alternative to the Middle East, described Chinese oil assertions as "one of the more astonishing episodes in the modern history of oil exploration".[110] He criticized Japanese optimism as "wishful thinking ... mistaken for a genuine critical forecasting", something flamed by "Japanese businessmen, the world press and quite a few Western China scholars..." as well as what he coins as influential scholarly publications.[111] Smil highlighted an example of what he considered to be an "astonishingly" bold Chinese deflection of their inability to meet Japanese oil demands through Vice-Premier Li Xiannian's communication to Keidanren's President Toshio Doko in October 1975 that "China could not supply as much crude oil as Japan wanted" and advised him instead to buy "more silk and other traditional Chinese products".[112]

Inflated expectations of Chinese oil potential were not entirely generated by the Chinese side. The Japanese were just as guilty of deliberate creative management of statistics in order to boost their bargaining position with the Organization of Petroleum Exporting Countries (OPEC) and in their eagerness to engage China economically.[113] Japanese leading representatives in the Sino-Japanese oil interactions like Ryotaro Hasegawa (chairperson of the board of Asian Oil which included a number of Japanese oil companies and trading firms) was among those who were most enthusiastic about Chinese oil production, upping his Chinese oil import figures from 350,000 tons of Chinese oil during the third quarter of 1974, to three to four million in the first half of 1975 to 10 million in the second half.[114]

His figure for Chinese oil production was just as optimistic, raising the figure of 50 million tons in 1973 to 70 million tons in 1974 and 100 million tons in 1975 and, placing supreme faith in the effectiveness

[110] Smil, V. (2004). *China's Past, China's Future Energy, Food, Environment*, p. 55. London: RoutledgeCurzon.

[111] Ibid., pp. 34-35.

[112] Ibid., p. 55.

[113] Hardy, R.W. (1978), p. 27.

[114] Wu, Y. (1977), p. 51.

of Japanese technical aid, he expected the figure to attain 400 million tons by 1980![115] Some argued that pressures for him to raise such highly optimistic figures arose from the fact that Japan was still recovering from the oil crisis and it needed greater bargaining power to negotiate with the Soviets for more oil.[116] By engaging simultaneously with the Chinese and Soviet Union, Japan hoped to secure oil from both communist suppliers, unaware that the Chinese were playing the same game as well. Consequently, both the Chinese and Japanese had similar intentions to raise their expectation of the Sino-Japanese oil trade vis-à-vis Soviet-Japanese oil trade although from opposite ends of the trilateral competition — the Chinese to discourage the Japanese from engaging with the USSR and the Japanese to persuade the Soviets to give them greater quantities and more affordable oil by citing the Chinese oil alternative.

By 1980, it was apparent that China could not meet the eight million tons quota of crude oil to Japan under the LTTA. The quotas were reduced by 13 percent and 45 percent respectively in the next two years and it remained at capped rates until 1985.[117] Japanese opponents of the LTTA (including oil refiners) were also skeptical of the quality of oil they were getting from the Chinese, disparaging it as low quality waxy crude oil.[118] According to Kim Woodard, sediment, water and residual oil content were also part of the problem.[119]

As early as 1975, Japanese users complained that Daqing crude had high paraffin content and began to press for price concessions.[120] Because of the waxy content of Chinese oil, Japanese balked at the extra costs of modifying or constructing new refineries to handle Chinese oil.[121] The wax content of Chinese oil required special refineries, cracking facilities and processes which Japan's refiners lacked up till the late 1970s and were reluctant to purchase these

---

[115] Ibid.

[116] Ibid.

[117] Newby, L. (1988), p. 23.

[118] Ibid., p. 8.

[119] Woodard, K. (1980), p. 128.

[120] Lieberthal, K. and Oksenberg, M. (1986), p. 184.

[121] Barnett, D.A. (1981), p. 464.

new technologies when they were spending money on facilities to de-sulphurize Middle Eastern Oil, their primary source of oil energy.[122]

The option of burning the crude as it is in Japanese power plants and steel mills was also considered.[123] In 1975, Japanese negotiators tried to lower the price of Daqing crude from the Chinese offer of US$12.10/bbl in February 1975 to US$9.01/bbl.[124] In all fairness, despite its low gasoline yield, Daqing crude had its advantages. On the upside, it has low sulfur content and could produce high quality kerosene and diesel oil; its particularly light diesel and residual fuel oil has low metal content that enabled Daqing crude to be directly fed into cracking units.[125]

China was also unable to meet its quota of eight million tons of crude to Japan in 1980.[126] At the same time, the 1980 export projection from the Japanese perspective fell from 100 to 50 and then 35 million tons.[127] Even so, momentum was kept with China's largest exports which was crude oil (40.9 percent of total exports) representing 5.2 percent of Japan's total petroleum imports.[128] Chinese crude exports to Japan reached a peak in 1985 at 350,000 barrels per day (b/d).[129] By 1986, the quality of oil became a major concern and contributed to Japan's reluctance to meet the projected quota of oil purchase under the LTTA (only 35–50 percent of the 1970s LTTA projections were met).[130]

The ideological power of Daqing fed the pride and exuberance of both China and Japan, leading them to over-promise and over-extend

[122] Hardy, R.W. (1978), p. 61.

[123] Woodard, K. (1980), p. 128.

[124] Ibid.

[125] Wang, H. H. (1999). *China's Oil Industry and Market*, p. 88. The Netherlands: Elsevier.

[126] Newby, L. (1988), p. 23.

[127] Woodard, K. (1980), p. 128.

[128] Hsu, I. C. Y. (2000). *The Rise of Modern China*. New York and Oxford: Oxford University Press.

[129] Wang, H. H. (1999), p. 25.

[130] Newby, L. (1988), p. 23.

their expectations, making the project unsustainable. Dissatisfaction with oil quality coupled with Japan's domestic diversification of energy sources led the Japanese to decrease orders for Chinese oil. As a result of the cutback in Japanese oil demand, the Chinese side also learnt about market capitalism the hard way, especially the vulnerability of a single commodity to global market forces. Both parties began to pull back from the irrational exuberance that seemed to characterize the early stages of the Sino-Japanese oil diplomacy during the 1970s oil crisis.

In 1981, they agreed that both sides would consult each other to determine the amount of additional crude oil to be exported from China to Japan after 1983.[131] This was the first sign that things were not going so well at a diplomatic level. To make matters worse, in 1985, the world economy experienced a glut in oil supplies. For the next 20 years, Japan's average annual growth rate in oil demand slowed to 2.7 percent between 1985–1995 and only 1.7 percent in the last five years of this period.[132] Correspondingly, Japan began to place a limit on its absorption rate of Chinese oil. Chinese oil exports to Japan tapered off to 230,000 b/d from 1995 to 1997.[133] The Chinese government, on the other hand, wanted to increase production to use volume to offset the drop in prices and thus, differences started to emerge. Both sides eventually settled on a compromised figure of 800,000 tons of Chinese oil supply to Japan.[134]

This phase was known as the "readjustment" period, a far calmer assessment of Sino-Japanese oil trade in comparison with what some saw as the irrational exuberance of 1977–1978. Parties involved in this trade realized that an annual Chinese oil production of 400 million tons was not possible.[135] To come up with more oil for exports, the Chinese adopted the "conservation"[136] policy or the "squeeze

---

[131] Ibid., p. 11.

[132] Horsnell, P. (1997), p. 23.

[133] Wang, H. H. (1999), p. 25.

[134] Newby, L. (1988), p. 23.

[135] Keith, R. C. (1986), p. 43.

[136] Ibid.

principle"[137] in response to falling oil production and inability to meet supply quotas to Japan and other customers to keep bilateral oil trade going. In the summer of 1980, conservation as an official policy was placed on the same footing as development.[138] The "squeeze principle" involved rationing domestic consumption of crude oil in order to maintain a sustainable level of exports to customers like Japan. This strategy enabled China to bring in much-needed foreign currency to buy foreign machinery and technologies while rationalizing Chinese energy consumption at the same time. Even in the mid-1980s, oil remained a valuable Chinese export, accounting for almost 25 percent of China's foreign exchange.[139] This was in line with the Chinese developmental doctrine of maintaining control over their own resources to sustain economic development on their own terms.[140]

POLITICAL CHALLENGES

During the Cultural Revolution corresponding to the early stages of Sino-Japanese oil contact, close affiliation to the Japanese became a weapon of choice for critics of the Petroleum Faction who accused some of its leaders of having suspect loyalty during the anti-Japanese war. Yu Qiuli, for example, was compelled by the conservatives to investigate Kang Shien's credentials during the war against Japan.[141] Kang defended himself by arguing that, from the early stages of the Sino-Japanese War, he had participated in anti-Japanese student rallies to the extent that he did not attend "a decent day of class (*meiyou zhengerbajingdi shangguo yitianke*)" in his own words.[142]

Yu also defended Kang and rejected such charges but, through this experience, the dangers of working with the Japanese in the oil

[137] Ibid., p. 20.
[138] Ibid., p. 44.
[139] Ibid., p. 22.
[140] Ibid., p. 20.
[141] Chen, D. K. (1994), p. 318.
[142] Ibid., p. 38.

trade became apparent. It brought back memories of attacks against Yu at the height of the Cultural Revolution when the level-headed Premier Zhou Enlai played a major role in protecting the Petroleum faction leader Yu Qiuli from incarceration by the Red Guards by arguing that Yu enjoyed Mao's confidence.[143] Using his political clout and proximity to Mao, Zhou had, in fact, quietly maintained production at China's Daqing oilfield.[144] In this manner, Zhou was the *de facto* guardian angel of the oil industry behind the scenes within the top Chinese leadership. His death exposed the Petroleum leaders to attacks by the conservatives.

At the height of the Cultural Revolution, other top Chinese leaders like Deng Xiaoping closely associated to the Petroleum faction were also in the process of being purged by the infamous Gang of Four led by Mao Zedong's widow. In January 1976, Deng was also attacked for his policies on equipment plant imports, accused of increasing China's balance-of-payments deficits in 1973–1974 while both Deng and Kang were attacked for exporting Chinese oil overseas.[145] Following Zhou Enlai's death on 8 January 1976, the anti-Petroleum faction Gang of Four moved to prevent Deng Xiaoping from taking up the post of Premier of China, removed him from office and then proceeded to reverse some of Deng's policy, including outreach to Japan.[146] On 10 February 1976, in a conference for officials from the provinces, municipalities and military regions, Zhang Chunqiao and his Shanghai supporter criticized Deng as a "comprador bourgeosie" and "more noxious than Chiang K'ai-shek (Jiang Jieshi)"; he was supported by Jiang Qing who added that "China's petroleum was all being taken off to other countries".[147]

The Gang of Four in the post-Mao era then tried to "sabotage" crude shipments to Japan in mid-February 1976 by cutting it down drastically to 250,000 metric tons from the monthly shipments of

143 Lieberthal, K. and Oksenberg, M. (1986), p. 67.

144 Ibid., p. 174.

145 Woodard, K. (1980), p. 131.

146 Lieberthal, K. and Oksenberg, M. (1986), p. 186.

147 Ibid.

600,000–700,000 tons to Japan.[148] The cut was so abrupt that Japanese tankers had to be recalled to port on their way to pick up Chinese crude.[149] In addition, there were reports and rumors that the Gang of Four Shanghai Radicals deliberately encouraged the burning of crude oil as fuel in electric power plants in Shanghai and Liaoning provinces instead of coal to reduce the stock of excess oil for export in a bid to sabotage Chinese oil exports.[150] These early attacks were brutal but the Faction survived when the Gang of Four was deposed.

After the Cultural Revolution, Sino-Japanese cooperation in Daqing was also affected by the deaths of China's paramount leaders, Zhou Enlai and Chairman Mao which unleashed a power struggle in the upper echelons of the Communist Party leadership. Although the anti-Petroleum Faction leaders were eventually defeated, political attacks on the Sino-Japanese oil trade persisted into the 1980s. With Japanese reluctance to absorb more oil, accusations began to fly from the Chinese side, e.g., the Japanese were more interested in selling them oil drilling machinery on the pretext of buying oil from China.[151] Moreover, the Chinese had constructed pipelines in anticipation of the oil trade with the Japanese, for example, from Daqing to Qinhuangdao and a parallel line from Daqing to Tiehling, with large diameter seamless steel pipes imported from Japan and constructed the lines themselves with little regards to costs.[152] Their understanding was to use revenues from the oil exports to Japan to pay for these constructions.[153] Thus, when the Japanese reduced their orders, the Chinese were caught with the huge outlay on investments.

With the drastic reduction in Japanese energy needs and an overall change in political climate, anti-Petroleum faction forces led by

---

148 Woodard, K. (1980), p. 129.

149 Ibid.

150 Ibid., p. 130.

151 Newby, L. (1988), p. 23.

152 Woodard, K. (1980), p. 141.

153 Ibid.

Chen Yun began to gain ground. This faction agitated for a slower pace of market reform and more meticulous assessment of China's own energy needs.[154] Chen's clique steadily gained ground starting from 1983, strengthened along the way by China's own frustrations at Japanese reactions to a volatile international energy market.[155] In addition, the PRC had accumulated trade deficits with Japan of some US$680 million in 1974, ballooning to US$1 billion in 1975 despite their attempts to finance increased imports through oil exports to Japan.[156] Because of the deficit and other issues, China decided to diversify its oil exports, downgrading Japan's proportion of its energy exports from 60 percent before 1983, to 51 percent in 1984 and 38 percent in 1985.[157]

The Petroleum Faction was then further weakened by the Bohai Incident, an industrial accident that happened at a Japanese-funded oil rig project, where many of their junior allies were demoted or replaced. This removed the support base for the Faction and made them weaker in resisting political reshuffles of the 1980s. At the ministerial level, Kang Shien was replaced by Wang Tao, an ally of Li Peng.[158] At the top of the politico-military bureaucratic hierarchy, Yu Qiuli was replaced by Yang Baibing as the head of PLA's General Political Department in 1988.[159] Yang Baibing belonged to a powerful faction of ex-Liu Shaoqi followers led by Yang Shangkun[160] while Li Peng's faction drew from ex-Zhou Enlai associates. Both Yang and Li factions were rivals of Hu Yaobang who belonged to the Deng Xiaoping faction that promoted the oil trade with Japan.

Meanwhile, General Secretary Hu Yaobang, widely seen as a pro-Japanese investment figure, abruptly resigned in 1987 due to domestic

---

[154] Newby, L. (1988), p. 25.

[155] Ibid.

[156] Hardy, R.W. (1978), p. 60.

[157] Lee, T. H. (1995), p. 213.

[158] Ibid., p. 71.

[159] Ibid., p. 66.

[160] Ibid., p. 57.

political reasons.[161] One of the speculated reasons for his departure was his "over-friendly" relations with Japan.[162] Hu was heavily criticized for inviting Japanese Prime Minister Yasuhiro Nakasone to a rare private family dinner in 1984.[163] Hu's actions were placed under Party scrutiny. In charges documented in Central Document No. 3 supported by party elders like Bo Yibo at an enlarged meeting of the Politburo on 16 January 1987, Hu was accused of "making unauthorized statements and taking unauthorized actions regarding foreign policy, such as inviting 3000 young Japanese to visit China".[164] Hu was compelled to go through a "self-criticism" session and resigned from the top party post.[165] In 1988, Acting Premier Li Peng backed up by Vice-Premier Yao Yilin advocated electric power over oil as the reigning priority for the Chinese energy industry.[166] Li was also keen to focus on rural energy and had led a rural energy group on 19 May 1984 supported by the China Rural Development Research Center.[167] When the State Council was restructured, Li became the Premier and the petroleum industry was integrated into the new Ministry of Energy Resources in April 1988.[168] The petroleum industry and its oil trade took a back seat to other rural energy projects.

Judging from the changes detailed above, both countries now have their own respective domestic priorities that are not necessarily mutually compatible. The relative permutations of benefits and detriments for the Chinese state and its Japanese counterpart have shifted and weakened over time. It had reached a point of time when the

---

[161] Newby, L. (1988), p. 29.

[162] Ibid., p. 65.

[163] Zhao, Q. (1996). *Interpreting Chinese Foreign Policy*, p. 163. Hong Kong: Oxford University Press.

[164] Ibid., p. 122.

[165] Ibid.

[166] Lee, T. (1995), p. 159.

[167] Keith, R. C. (1986), p. 48.

[168] Lee, T. H. (1995), p. 160.

Chinese state was not able to bargain any more, nor could it overcome the bargaining strength of the opposite party, e.g., inability to convince the Japanese to accept more Chinese oil imports due to the former's successes in conservation policies. Sino-Japanese bilateral trade in oil began to slow down.

Chapter 8

Conclusion

In evaluating Daqing, Kenneth Lieberthal who wrote a detailed report on bureaucratic politics in the Chinese oil industry quoted Frederick Teiwes' theory of the bandwagon effect[1] to describe political and industrial decision-making in the Maoist era — that China's top leaders and bureaucracy made a professional career out of anticipating and reading Mao's thoughts and the direction in which he was leaning towards. The first ones to read the mind correctly jumps onto the bandwagon to get an early ride to success while those that read his mind wrongly or were purposely misled by Mao faced dire consequences including purges and imprisonment. In some ways, overwhelming enthusiasm generated by Daqing's initial successes and the subsequent rapid fall of Daqing-ism seemed to confirm this theory.

The complex aspirations for the Daqing project proceeded unproblematically until the Cultural Revolution when Daqing revealed the fissures in the uneasy relationship/partnership between

[1] Lieberthal, K. (2004). *Governing China*, p. 85. New York and London: WW Norton & Company.

Communist ideological orthodoxy and non-proletariat specialist bourgeois technocracy. Mao suddenly realized that Daqing was an entrenchment of what he wanted otherwise, which was constant renewals in the bureaucracy to prevent the stifling of revolutionary fervor and a desire to erase any semblance of Old China's hierarchical stratified society.

Between 1966 and 1969, Daqing lost Mao's favor and did not feature high in his mental landscape and was abandoned as a solution to his anxieties.[2] Daqing, the Petroleum Faction and the entire petroleum industry became marginal to Mao's concerns, and, hence, they were potentially dispensable in the political scene. The Petroleum Faction savored their place in the sun for a period of time but this all came to an end when Mao's privileges and favor for Daqing were withdrawn. The delicate and perhaps uneasy relationship between the hardcore ideologues of Chinese politics and the progressive technocrats which had endured up till now broke down. In 1967, Japanese observers in China noted the appearance of a newspaper circulated in Daqing which accused the Daqing Party Committee of operating the oilfield like a "private kingdom" and misleading Mao and the Central Committee about the activities that went on at Daqing.[3]

This episode demonstrated that the material and ideological facets of Daqing were indistinguishable and ideological approval of the project was intrinsic to its continued success and progress. Daqing's fate indicated that conceptualizations and ideas about the project was not a timeless and immutable constant and instead represented the instrumentalism in the inventions of specific historical moments. It evolved through a process of invention and reinvention of ideas about Daqing, a constant creative destruction process to bring it closer and make it more relevant to dominant ideological ideas of the day. As if to prove this right, the reinstatement of the technocracy in the post-Cultural Revolution period was as swift and certain as their eradication.

---

[2] Lieberthal, K. and Oksenberg, M. (1986), p. 174.

[3] Chan, L.W. (1974), p. 12.

Despite the characterization of the 1958–1978 period as the "lost decades",[4] China in fact achieved remarkable progress towards self-reliance in this period in the oil industry. Dependent on oil imports in all of its modern history, the People's Republic of China finally became self-reliant in petroleum production in the mid-1960s and started to export modest amounts in the early 1970s and by the mid-1980s.[5] The PRC whittled down the dependency rate for foreign machinery imports and increased its self-sufficiency rate from 35 percent in 1953–1957 to 80 percent between 1960–1974.[6] Just as importantly, China's progress in the oil industry served as a morale booster in the often tumultuous early years of the PRC.

Fortunately for the Chinese oil industry, the dense network of technocrats and their supporters as well as PLA elites helped the Petroleum Faction and Daqing tide over these tumultuous times as Daqing re-emerged in the post-Cultural Revolution period to achieve another milestone — which is its exposure to international trade that was examined in the chapter on Sino-Japanese oil interactions. To re-engage the international community and particularly Japan, China's first major oil client, a re-configuration of the concept of self-reliance was undertaken.

Deng Xiaoping made a magnificent comeback in July 1977 and became Vice-Premier and vice-chairperson of the Chinese Communist Party (CCP). With stabilized levels of oil production, paramount leader Deng Xiaoping gave Daqing and the Chinese oil industry a new direction again on the eve of a national gathering (*Shijie Sanzhong Quanhui*) on 14 September 1978 and said: "You have to speed up your search for oil and gas and look for more oil and gas fields. We already have 500 million tons of oil and getting another ten Daqings is not easy indeed!".[7]

The government also hinted at a re-orientation of emphasis on maintaining high levels of production (*gaochan, wenchan*)[8] at the

---

[4] Smil, V. (1976), p. xii.

[5] Lieberthal, K. and Oksenberg, M. (1986), p. 151.

[6] Cheng, C. (1976), p. 112.

[7] Wen, *et al.* (2002), p. 438.

[8] Ibid.

existing oilfields like Daqing. This message was picked up by Deng's apparent successor at that time, Party Secretary General Hu Yaobang who proposed: "First, it is crucial to determine the volume of stable oil production and exploitation in the contributions that Daqing makes to our country. Second, it is to open up new oil regions and a new front in the battle for oil. If we cannot find a Daqing, perhaps we can try looking for a medium-sized Daqing or several mini-Daqings. And third to develop our petrochemical industry".[9]

Expansion of production necessitated a radical upgrading of technological capability and equipment. Western observers of Chinese oil industry like Vaclav Smil evaluated Chinese oil equipment and found them to be at least two decades behind their Western contemporaries.[10] Japan's outreach in the area of energy cooperation was met positively in the period between 1964–1966 (before the onset of the Cultural Revolution), a period which some analysts characterized as the "second wave of import policy" (the first being Soviet help between 1956–1960.[11]

During the Cultural Revolution interregnum, to counter the conservatives' rise, the pioneers that pushed for export of China's resources to foreign countries like Japan fought the conservatives by basing their arguments on economics in the late 1970s.[12] The Petroleum faction now led by Vice-Premiers Li Xiannian and Gu Mu won a major argument against their rivals by highlighting the virtues of catering to an expansion of the international energy export market.[13] Exporting energy resources was also needed to absorb foreign currency needed to purchase technological goods for China's modernization.[14] This was not a new argument and can in fact be traced to precedents enunciated by former generations of Petroleum faction leaders. In the Sino-Japanese rapprochement period, Petroleum faction leader Kang Shien pushed forward opening up of the Chinese oil

[9] Ibid.

[10] Smil, V. (1976), p. 96.

[11] Lee, T. H. (1995), p. 198.

[12] Newby, L. (1988), p. 25.

[13] Ibid.

[14] Ibid.

industry and became the evangelist for technological innovation in China and of expanding contact with foreign trading partners like Japan to develop China's resources.[15]

These arguments slowly beat the Gang of Four into retreat along with other factors which led to their demise. Starved of advanced foreign technologies and technical training, China was poised to go on a technology-buying spree (including oil equipment) in a bid to catch up with the rest of the world. With enthusiasm for conducting oil trade boosted by favorable domestic conditions and political will on both sides generated by an oil-crisis-hit energy-paranoid Japan and a foreign reserve-starved post-Cultural Revolution China, Sino-Japanese oil interactions took off from 1978 when China formally emerged from the turbulent Cultural Revolutions under the leadership of Hua Guofeng and Deng Xiaoping. In 1978, her exports to overseas oil customers, of which Japan is a main component, hit double-digit million tons for the first time.

SINO-JAPANESE RELATIONS

Sino-Japanese oil relations were characterized by permeability, ambiguity and interdependence underpinned by the pragmatic construct (separation of economics and politics) of the energy trade as a neutral space, one that is relatively less burdened by rhetorical disagreements over war memories. Because oil was often in demand, it also served as a non-threatening and convenient political excuse for initiating Sino-Japanese relations and both parties were aware of this. In addition, heavy industries like petroleum extraction and processing required the involvement of governmental capital and bureaucratic support, making it convenient as an item to slip into governmental exchanges under the hood of semi-official or private sector communications, constructing an interactive platform for political and economic activities.

When China achieved self-reliance in the 1960s, it was in a position of exporting oil and this role was aided by Japanese receptiveness

[15] Lieberthal, K. and Oksenberg, M. (1986), p. 24.

towards trading in the commodity with China after the 1972 Nixon rapprochement. Since the 1960s with the discovery of Daqing, Chinese corporations set up in dealing with the material resource have been almost exclusively governmental. With the Nixon rapprochement in 1972, state firms started to get their first experiences in working with non-state actors. For example, Japanese firms were amongst the first to work with Chinese oil state firms. At this time, Japanese companies were compelled by circumstances to work with the Chinese government because of the 1973 oil cartel embargo following the Arab-Israeli conflicts. Estimates during this period which pegged total Chinese petroleum volume at two to six billion tons made the prospects of Chinese oil particularly enticing.[16]

The IDE-JETRO publication *Chugoku no Sekiyuu to Tenran Gasu* (*China's Oil and Natural Gas*) proclaimed Japan's foreign exchange for China's Daqing's crude as something "valuable (*kichou* also translatable to treasure)"[17] obtained by China, perhaps boosting Japan's capacity-building status and forgetting its own benefits from the deal such as her appetite for raw materials and fuels from China, including eight to nine million tons of coal and 47.1 million tons of crude oil.[18] Most importantly, Japan needed to sustain her momentum for double digit economic growth which had been threatened by the oil crisis.

Along with the post-Cultural Revolution agenda of expanding oil production, the oil industry henceforth would not merely serve as a fountainhead of Chinese industrialization but was modified to "expand the international influence of China's large enterprises overseas (*guangda zhongguo daqiye zai guojishang de yingxiang*)" and to let them "compete and struggle to let socialist enterprises get a foothold in the highly-competitive international market".[19] Domestically, Daqing

---

[16] Rothenberg, M. (1977), p. 123.

[17] Tatsu, K. (2002), p. 31.

[18] Newby, L. (1988), p. 7.

[19] Guojia Tongjiju Gongjiaoshi (National Statistical Bureau) and Xinhuashe Guoneibu Gongye Bianjishi (Xinhua News Agency National Industries Editorial Department) (1990), pp. 1 and 5.

seems to have served its purpose "instilling patriotic spirit within the Chinese people, establishing self-reliance, displaying imprints of heroism",[20] etc.

Outwardly, the Chinese oil industry and Daqing needed to achieve the same sterling reputation in production performance as they did domestically and the opportunity arrived when its crude was exported to Japan to yield foreign currency. Outward-looking export-orientation perhaps also fitted in well with China's aspirations to be a model for the developing world. In line with the ideal of modernization theories, the oil industry's industrial achievements quantified with glowing figures were touted as a successful enterprise that was famous both "within and outside China *(chiming zhongwai)*".[21]

Japan would become the main recipient of Chinese oil from this invigorated export drive while China became the largest recipient of Japanese Official Development Assistance (ODA) from 1982 to 1986 and second largest from 1987 to 1992 (except 1991).[22] Between 1979 to 1995, there were three major provisions of Japanese yen soft loans worth US$1.5 billion (or 350 billion yen between 1979 and 1984), US$2.1 billion (or 470 billion yen between 1985 and 1990) and US$5.4 billion (or 810 billion yen between 1990 and 1995).[23] Up to that point of time, these were the biggest loans that China had ever received, more than the US$1.5 billion loan from the socialist Eastern European bloc between 1953 and 1960.[24] Japan was the first non-Communist government to forward the PRC loans.[25]

The willingness on the part of the PRC to take such loans despite a longstanding self-imposed restriction of not owing money to former imperialists of their homelands also demonstrated a level of comfort, understanding and friendship they had towards Japan. Japanese

[20] Ibid., p 13.
[21] Ibid., p. 12.
[22] Zhao, Q. (1996), p. 151.
[23] Ibid., pp. 152–153.
[24] Lee, C. (1984), p. 113.
[25] Zhao, Q. (1996), p. 157.

technical experts in China also took over the status of the country with the largest number of foreign expertise in China since Soviet help before the Sino-Soviet split; 40 percent of the total number of 10,000 foreign experts in China were Japanese citizens by 1986.[26] In this way, Chinese openness to Japanese collaboration was partly technical in nature. Ever since Daqing and other oilfields were discovered, Chinese exploitation was limited by the laggard state of its petroleum equipment industry which was also a major factor accounting for the PRC being a minor exporter of oil in the early 1970s.[27]

Japanese views represented by the IDE-JETRO publication *Chugoku no Sekiyuu to Tenran Gasu* (*China's Oil and Natural Gas*) tended to view China's oil exports as being mutually exclusive or even antithetical to the doctrine of self-reliance. In other words, the policy of "*jili gengsheng* (self-reliance)" was seen as being ousted by "*duiwai kaifang* (open to the outside world)" policy.[28] To Chinese understanding, this was not necessarily so. Export of energy resources was needed to absorb foreign currency needed to purchase technological goods for China's modernization.[29] In the purchase of technologies from overseas, China in fact focused on turnkey projects and technological transfers which would allow her to build up her own self-reliant industrial capabilities in the process. This aspect was crucial for increasing her oil exports.

Even at a time of increased oil exports, China was gradually opening up to imports of oil, contradicting the portrayal of the Chinese oil industry in the heyday of Daqing euphoria as the "new Saudi Arabia".[30] This was a time when renowned academicians like Kim Woodard highlighted the rumors that China would overtake the USSR

---

[26] Ibid., p. 162.

[27] Rawski, T. G. (1980), p. 64.

[28] Tatsu, K. (2002), p. 36.

[29] Newby, L. (1988), p. 25.

[30] Smil, V. (2004), p. 9.

and the US in energy production shortly after 1980.[31] In that period, the International Energy Agency (IEA) admitted that experts suggested that the most promising Chinese hydrocarbon reserves could surpass that of Saudi Arabia.[32] It was a period of great optimism, one that had to be understood in its own context.

Under the twin pressures of increasing Chinese oil exports and foreign oil imports, the Chinese leadership rationalized that self-reliance did not have to mean only isolating oneself from the international community but that foreign capital and investments could be subjugated and disciplined by the state without compromising the state's control and autonomy over a strategic vital resource like oil. China's oil industry had shifted from being inward-looking strategic state enterprises to government-linked import/export trading companies with an open door policy. The planned strategy was to consolidate their operations to compete more effectively in international competition with foreign oil companies and to open up to collaborations with foreign firms for opportunities in oil exports.

Between the 1980s and 1997, Chinese oil development went through a hybridized phase. Internationalization initiatives carried out in the late 1970s in line with China's opening economy necessitated institutional privatization to handle and manage its assets. The Chinese oil firms themselves took steps to adjust and adapt to less state reliance and become more reactive to market forces. Internationalization stimulated reforms to make China's petrochemical firms internationally competitive.

In essence, market competition, not imperialism, war or ideology, became the main driving force for the adaptation of science and technology. Energy mobilization was now predicated upon catching up and competing with the world's "technically-concentrated enterprises and multinationals" that "have significantly increased investment in the

---

[31] Woodard, K. (1980), p. 5.

[32] International Energy Agency (2000). *China's Worldwide Quest for Energy Security*, p. 23. France: International Energy Agency.

intangible assets so that knowledge and technology hold the key to the corporate development".[33] Summing up the new priorities succinctly, China's Petroleum Industry Press urged "Chinese oil giants to implement technical innovation and talented strategies so as to rank themselves among the large international oil companies".[34]

[33] Liu, Z., Fang, C. and Wang, T. (chief eds.) (2003). *Outlook of High-Tech Application in Petroleum Industry* (*Gaoxin Jishu Zai Shiyou Gongyezhong de Shiyong*), preface. Beijing: Petroleum Industry Press (*Shiyou Gongye Chubanshe*).
[34] Ibid.

Bibliography

Ajia Tsushinsha (Asia News Agency) (1963). *Chugoku Sangyou Boeki Souran (An Index of China's Industries and Trade)*. Japan: Ajia Tsushinsha (Asia News Agency).

Barnett, D. A. (1981). *China's Economy in Global Perspective.* Washington DC: The Brookings Institution.

Bartke, W. (1977). *Oil in the People's Republic of China.* Montreal: McGill-Queens University Press.

Beijing Chubanshe (1966). *Xiang Daqingshi Qiye Xuexi (Learn from Daqing-style Industries)*. Beijing: Beijingchubanshe.

Bernardo, R. M. (1977). *Popular Management and Pay in China.* Quezon City, Philippines: University of the Philippines Press.

CIA (1977). *China: Oil Production Prospects.* ER 77-100 OU.

Center of International Studies, Princeton University (1981). *The Modernization of China*. Rozman, G. (ed.). New York and London: The Free Press.

Chan, L. W. (1974). *The Taching Oilfield: A Maoist Model for Economic Development Contemporary China Papers No. 8.* Australia: Australian National University Press.

Chen, D. K. (1994). *Zhongguo Shiyou Dahui Zhan (A Chinese Great Battle for Oil)*. China: Bayi Chubanshe.

Cheng, C. (1976). *China's Petroleum Industry.* New York: Praeger.

Daqing Wenhua Yishuguan (Daqing Arts and Culture Museum) (1976). *Daqing Suxie Xuanji (Selected Works of Daqing Sketches)*. Heilongjiang: Heilongjiang Renmin Chubanshe.

Daqing Youtian Gongren Xiezhuozu (The Writers' Team for Daqing) (1971). *Daqingren de Gushi (Story of the People at Daqing)*. Shanghai: Shanghai Renmin Chubanshe (Shanghai People's Publishing House).

Daqing Youtian Tieren Xuexiao Dangzhibu (Daqing Oilfield Ironman School Party Branch) (1977). Yong Daqing Jingshen ban Xuexiao Peiyang Tierenshi de Jiebanren (Using the Daqing Spirit to Manage a School to Produce Ironman-like Successors). In *Gongye Zhanxian de Xianyan Hongqi (The Brightly-Colored Red Flag of the Industrial Battlefront)*. China: Renminchubanshe.

Department of State (1967). *The China White Paper August 1949 Volume II. Originally Issued as United States Relations with China with Special Reference to the Period 1944–1949. Department of State Publication 3573. Far Eastern Series 30.* Stanford California: Stanford University Press.

Downs, E. S. (2000). *China's Quest for Energy Security.* Prepared for the United States Airforce. California and Virginia: RAND.

Falconer, A. (1950). *New China Friend or Foe?* Beijing: Foreign Languages Press.

Foreign Language Teaching and Research Press (2002). *New Century Chinese-English Dictionary*. Singapore: Foreign Language Teaching and Research Press and Learners Publishing.

Foreign Languages Press (1977). *The National Conference on Learning from Taching in Industry Selected Documents*. Beijing: Foreign Languages Press.

Gaimusho Keizaikyoku Keizaitogoka (Japan's Ministry of Foreign Affairs Economics Bureau Economics Statistics Section) (1970). *Chugoku Tariku no Shigen to Chukyo no Shigen Seisaku (Mainland China's Resources and Chinese Communist Party's Resource Policies)*. Japan: Gaimusho Keizaikyoku Keizaitogoka (Japan's Ministry of Foreign Affairs Economics Bureau Economics Statistics Section).

Garth, A. (1973). *The Invisible China: The Overseas Chinese and the Politics of Southeast Asia*. New York: Macmillan.

Gasster, M. (1972). *China's Struggle to Modernize.* New York: Alfred A. Knopf.

Goldstein, S. M. (1992). The CCP's Foreign Policy of Opposition, 1937-1945. In *China's Bitter Victory. The War with Japan 1937-1945*. Hsiung J. C. and Levine, S. I. (eds.). New York and England: East Gate Book ME Sharpe.

Guangdongshen Geming Weiyuanhui Gongshe Bangongshi/Zhengzhibu (The Guangdong Revolutionary Committee Administration and Political Affairs Bureaus) (1973). *Zoudaqingde Daolu Bandaqingshi Qiye (Walk the Path of Daqing and Carry Out Daqing-style Industries)*. China: Guangdong Renmin Chubanshe.

Guojia Tongjiju Gongjiaoshi (National Statistical Bureau) and Xinhuashe Guoneibu Gongye Bianjishi (Xinhua News Agency National Industries Editorial Department) (1990). *Zhongguo Teda Qiye Zhuanlue (A Brief Biography of China's Extra Large Enterprises)*. China: Hualingchubanshe.

Hardy, R. W. (1978). *China's Oil Future: A Case of Modest Expectations.* Colorado: Westview Press.

Horsnell, P. (1997). *Oil in Asia.* UK: Oxford University Press for the Oxford Institution for Energy Studies.

Hsu, I. C. Y. (2000). *The Rise of Modern China.* New York and Oxford: Oxford University Press.

International Energy Agency (2000). *China's Worldwide Quest for Energy Security.* France: International Energy Agency.

Iriye, A. (1992). *China and Japan in the Global Setting.* Cambridge: Harvard University Press.

Jain, R. K. (1977). *China and Japan 1949-1976.* India: Humanities Press of New Jersey.

Jentleson, B. (1986). *Pipeline Politics.* Ithaca and London: Cornell University Press.

Jingjibu (Ministry of Economic Affairs), Republic of China (1971). *Dalu Feiqu Changkuang Gailan (General View of the Industries in Mainland China), Volume 1, Restricted.* Taiwan: Jingjibu.

Kang, S. Huainian Jignaide Zhou Enlai Tongzhi (Reminiscing the Beloved Comrade Zhou Enlai). In *Jiannan Chuangye Zhongguo Shiyou Gongye Dierji (The Difficulties of Starting an Industry: The Chinese*

Oil Industry Series Two), Jing, Z. (ed.). Beijing: Shiyou Gongye Chubanshe.

Kapelinsky, Y. N. (1959). *Development of the Economy and the Foreign Economic Contracts of the People's Republic of China*. NY: CCM Information Corporation.

Keith, R. C. (1986). China's Resource Diplomacy and National Energy Policy. In *Energy, Security and Economic Development in East Asia*. Keith, R. C. (ed.). NY: St Martin's Press.

Kitaoka, S. (1992). Diplomacy and the Military in Showa Japan. In *Showa. The Japan of Hirohito*. Gluck, C. and Graubard, S. R. (eds.). New York and London: WW Norton and Company.

Lee, C. (1984). *China and Japan New Economic Diplomacy.* Stanford California: Stanford University and Hoover Institution Press.

Lee, T. H. (1995). *Politics of Energy Policy in Post-Mao China*. Korea: Asiatic Research Center Korea University.

Li, C. (1977). *Yi 'Lianglun' Wei Zhidao, Jiansheguodeying de Jichendui (Using the 'Two Theories' as Guidance, To Build a Solid Grassroot Team*). China: Renminchubanshe.

Lieberthal, K. (2004). *Governing China.* New York and London: WW Norton & Company.

Lieberthal, K. and Oksenberg, M. (1986). *Bureaucratic Politics and Chinese Energy Development.* The University of Michigan Prepared for the Department of Commerce Contract No. 50-SATA-4-16230, Washington: Center for Chinese Studies.

Ling, H. C. (1975). *The Petroleum Industry of the People's Republic of China.* Stanford: Hoover Institution Press.

Liu, M. (1979). *Laojunmiao de Gushi* (*The Story of Laojunmiao*). Taipei: Huaqiao Wenhua Chubanshe.

Liu, Z., Fang, C. and Wang, T. (chief eds.) (2003). *Outlook of High-Tech Application in Petroleum Industry* (*Gaoxin Jishu Zai Shiyou Gongyezhong de Shiyong*). Beijing: Petroleum Industry Press (*Shiyou Gongye Chubanshe*).

Lowell, D. (1974). *Liu Shao-ch'i and the Chinese Cultural Revolution*. Berkeley, LA and London: University of California Press.

Newby, L. (1988). *Sino-Japanese Relations*. London: Routledge.

Ogata, S. (1988). *Normalization with China*. Berkeley: Institute of East Asian Studies University of California — Berkeley.

Okabe,A. (1986). *Sekiyu (Oil)*. Japan: Nihon Keizai Hyouronsha.

PLA Daily (2004) PLA Figures http://64.233.161.104/search?q=cache: Nso0okcSdzwJ:english.pladaily.com.cn/special/figures/zj/yql.htm+Daqing+PLA&hl=en, 5 May 2004.

Paik, K. W. (1995). *Gas and Oil in Northeast Asia*. Great Britain: The Royal Institute of International Affairs.

Park, C. (1975). *Energy Policies of the World: China.* Newark Delaware; Center for the Study of Marine Policy.

Prybyla, J. S. (1978). *The Chinese Economy.* Columbia: University of South Carolina Press.

Qiu, Z. (1999). Songliao Zhaoqi Dezhi Zhonghe Yanjiu Gongzhuo Jishi (Records of Early Consolidated Research Work at the Songliao Plains). In *Dangdai Zhongguo Youqi Kantan Zhongda Faxian (The Important Discoveries of Contemporary China's Oil and Gas Exploration*). Zhang, W. (ed.). Beijing: Shiyou Gongye Chubanshe.

Rawski, T. G. (1980). *China's Transition to Industrialism*. Ann Arbor: The University of Michigan Press.

Reichauer, E. O. (1988). *Japan: The History of a Nation.* New York: Alfred A. Knopf.

Renmin Chubanshe (1977). *Zhongguo Gongchangdang Zhongyang Weiyuan-hui Fuzhuxi Ye Jianying Tongzhi Xai Quanguo Gongye Xuedaqinghuishang De Jianghua (The Speech Given by Vice Chairman Comrade Ye Jianying at the National Chinese Communist Party Central Committee Learn from Daqing Conference*). Beijing: Renmin Chubanshe.

Richman, B. M. (1969). *Industrial Society in Communist China*. New York: Vintage Books.

Rothenberg, M. (1977). *Whither China: The View From the Kremlin*. Washington DC: International Affairs Center for Advanced International Studies Monograph. University of Miami.

Schmitter, P. C. Still the Century of Corporatism? In *Modernity Critical Concepts Volume III Modern Systems.* Waters, M. (ed.). London and New York: Routledge.

Shapiro, J. (2001). *Mao's War Against Nature.* New York: Cambridge University Press.

Sheldon, G. (1997). *Molding Japanese Minds.* New Jersey: Princeton.

Shi, B. (1999). *Zhongguo Shiyou Tianranqi Zhiyuan (China's Oil and Natural Gas Resources).* Beijing: Shiyou Gongye Chubanshe.

Smil, V. (1976). *China's Energy.* NY: Praeger Publishers.

Smil, V. (1988). *Energy in China's Modernization:Advances and Limitation.* Armonk, New York/London: East Gate Book ME Sharpe.

Smil, V. (1990). China's Energy:Advances and Limitations. In *Energy in China.* Desai, A.V. (ed.). New Delhi: International Development Research Centre and United Nations University.

Smil, V. (2004). *China's Past, China's Future Energy, Food, Enivronment.* London: Routledge Curzon.

Song, Z. (1977). 'Gaoju Mao Zedong de Weida Qizhi, Zou Woguo Zhiji Gongye (Raise the Majestic Flag of Mao Zedong. *Walk the Path of Our Indigenous Industries.* In *Gongye Zhanxian de Xianyan Hongqi (The Brightly-Colored Red Flag of the Industrial Battlefront).* China: Renminchubanshe.

Spence, J. (1999). *The Search for Modern China.* NY and London, WW Norton and Company.

State Statistical Bureau (ed.) (1983). *Zhongguo tongji nianjian (China Statistical Yearbook).* Beijing: Chinese Statistical Press.

Takashi, K. *Shigen Enerugicho (Japan's Department of Energy and Resources).* Japan: Kyouikukai Gyousei Series 15 (Japan Administrative Series 15).

Tatsu, K. (2002). *Chugoku no Sekiyuu to Tenran Gasu (China's Oil and Natural Gas).* Japan: Institute of Development Economies.

Thomson, E. (2001). *China's Growing Dependence on Oil Imports EAI Background Brief No. 87.* Singapore: East Asian Institute.

US Department of Energy (1981). *Energy Industries Abroad DOE/IA-0012 September 1981.* US: US Department of Energy prepared by Office of International Affaris.

US Government Printing Office (1974). *Committee on Foreign Affairs, Oil and Asian Rivals.* Hearings Before the Subcommittee on Asian and Pacific Affairs of the Committee on Foreign Affairs: House of Representatives 93rd Congress First and Second Sessions 12 September 1973; 30 January

6, 20 February, and 6 March (1974). Washington: US Government Printing Office.

Wang, H. H. (1999). *China's Oil Industry and Market*. The Netherlands: Elsevier.

Wang, Y. (1992). *Zhongguo Shiyou Shihua (About the History of China's Oil Industry)*. China: Shiyou Gongye Chubanshe.

Wen, H., Wang, Z., Zhang, J., Guan, X., Liu, M., Chen, Z., Dai. N., Nan, Y., Wu, Q., Zhang, S. and Wang, S. (2002). *Bainian Shiyou (100 Years of Petroleum)* (1878–2000). China: Dangdai Zhongguo Chubanshe.

Wong, J. and Wong, C. K. (1998). *China's New Oil Development Strategy Taking Shape*. Singapore: World Scientific.

Woodard, K. (1980). *The International Energy Relations of China*. California: Stanford University Press.

Wu, T. (1983). *Lin Biao and the Gang of Four*. Carbondale and Edwardsville: Southern Illinois University Press.

Wu, Y. (1977). *Japan's Search for Oil*. Stanford California: Stanford University.

Yang, J. (1999). Daqing Youtian de Faxian Guocheng (The Chronology of the Discovery of the Daqing Oilfield). In *Dangdai Zhongguo Youqi Kantan Zhongda Faxian (The Important Discoveries of Contemporary China's Oil and Gas Exploration)*. Zhang, W. (ed.). Beijing: Shiyou Gongye Chubanshe.

Yergin, D. (1991). *The Prize. The Epic Quest for Oil, Money and Power*. NY: Simon and Schuster.

Yu, Q. (1996). *Yu Qiuli Huiyilu (Memoirs of Yu Qiuli)*. Beijing: Jiefangjun Chubanshe. The PLA Press.

Zhang, D. D. (1997). *Transformation in the Political Economy of China's Relations with Japan in the Reform Era Pacific. Economic Papers No. 265*. Canberra: Australia-Japan Research Centre.

Zhang, J. (2004). *Catch-up and Competitiveness in China*. London and New York: RoutledgeCurzon.

Zhang, S. (1988). *Yumen Youkuangshi (A History of Yumen Oil Field) 1939–1949.* China: Xibei Daxue Chubanshe Xibei University Press.

Zhang, W. (1999). Zhongguo Shiyou Kantan Zhanlue Dongyi de Zhongda Tupo (The Great Breakthrough Behind Chinese Oil Exploration's Shift Eastwards). In *Dangdai Zhongguo Youqi Kantan Zhongda Faxian (The Important Discoveries of Contemporary China's Oil and Gas Exploration)*. Zhang, W. (ed.). Beijing: Shiyou Gongye Chubanshe.

Zhao, Q. (1996). *Interpreting Chinese Foreign Policy*. Hong Kong: Oxford University Press.

Zhonggong Daqing Youtian Disan Yiyuan Weiyuanhui (The Chinese Communist Party Daqing Oilfield No. 3 Hospital Committee) (1977). Shenru Kaizhan Weisheng Geming Yong Daqing Jingshen Ban Yiyuan (To Thoroughly Launch a Revolution in Health Using the Daqing Spirit to Manage a Hospital). In *Gongye Zhanxian de Xianyan Hongqi (The Brightly-Colored Red Flag of the Industrial Battlefront)*. China: Renminchubanshe.

Zhongguo Lianyou Gongye (China Oil-Refining Industry) Editorial Team (1989). *Zhongguo Lianyou Gongye (China Oil-Refining Industry)*. China: Shiyou Gongye Chubanshe.

Zhu, Y. (1990). Demand, Supply and Economics of Energy in China. In *Energy in China*. Desai, A. V. (ed.). New Delhi: International Development Research Centre and United Nations University.

Index

1973 25, 28, 31, 44, 45, 69, 73, 93, 95, 116, 121-123, 126-130, 133, 137, 140, 145, 156

automobile 122

barrels 30, 122, 142

catching up 38, 93, 109, 115, 159
China 1, 2, 4-8, 10-12, 14, 17-19, 21, 24, 25, 27, 29-31, 33-37, 39-41, 43-46, 49, 53, 54, 57-71, 73, 74, 76, 77, 79, 80, 82, 85, 87-92, 94, 95, 98-102, 106-111, 113, 115-119, 121-148, 151-160
coal 12, 16, 21, 108, 113, 122, 123, 146, 156
conferences 5, 26, 66, 93, 107
crude oil 2, 18, 66, 67, 69, 72, 113, 116, 129, 131, 134, 140-144, 146, 156

Daqing 1-6, 8-55, 57-59, 61, 63, 66-70, 72-76, 78, 80, 81-106, 108, 111-115, 118, 126-131, 133-135, 137, 138, 141, 142, 145, 146, 151-154, 156-158
Daqingism 96
dependence 4, 22, 44, 65, 68, 69, 90, 117, 123
diplomatic 65, 124, 127, 132, 143
Discovery 2-4, 10-12, 16, 17, 29, 30, 43, 50, 51, 63, 66, 67, 98, 106, 111, 156
distilling 75
drilling 14, 17, 20, 23, 26, 39, 42, 44, 46, 47, 55, 72, 75, 86, 134, 146

economic 3, 4, 7, 11, 12, 34, 63-66, 69, 73, 80, 82, 92, 93, 105, 108, 115, 118, 119, 122-124, 127, 132, 134-136, 138, 139, 144, 155, 156
economy 3, 7, 8, 11, 19, 21, 31, 35, 38, 68, 69, 72, 95, 111, 115, 122, 123, 143, 159
energy 2, 11, 19, 30, 62, 63, 71, 73, 86, 90, 91, 107-109, 111-114, 116, 118, 122-125, 132, 133, 137, 142-144, 146-148, 154, 155, 158, 159
equipment 1, 7, 8, 14, 20, 41, 42, 44, 70, 72-77, 109-111, 113-115, 130, 135, 145, 154, 155, 158
extraction 17, 31, 45, 58, 67, 69, 76, 78, 86, 109, 111, 116, 155

flooding 111, 112
foreign 4-8, 13, 20, 21, 24, 25, 31, 39, 40, 43, 44, 54, 57, 60-72, 74, 77, 78, 85, 107-111, 113-118, 121, 123, 125, 126, 128, 132, 133, 137, 139, 140, 144, 148, 153-159
fuels 63, 113, 156

government 7, 11, 14, 21, 24, 39, 59, 63, 65, 67, 78, 101, 102, 104, 124, 128, 130, 138, 143, 153, 156, 157, 159
Gross National Product (GNP) 114, 123
guerilla 13, 51, 80

ideological 3, 11, 28, 33, 34-37, 42, 48, 49, 55, 59, 63, 67, 68, 80-82, 84, 91-96, 99, 104, 109, 115, 116, 136, 142, 152
ideology 6, 8, 38, 48, 59, 60, 66, 83, 92, 96, 159
import 44, 116, 124, 126, 129, 130, 133, 138, 140, 154, 159
industrialization 1, 53, 67-69, 81, 83, 92, 98, 102, 109, 115, 118, 125, 156
infrastructure 21, 111, 115, 131

Japan 8, 60, 72, 107-109, 113-116, 118, 119, 121-138, 140-148, 153-157

Liao-Takasaki Memorandum 123
loans 7, 131, 133-135, 138, 139, 157
Long Term Trade Agreement (LTTA) 118, 119, 134, 135, 139, 141, 142

military 5, 14, 15, 22, 41, 50-54, 65, 66, 89-92, 97, 114, 145, 147
Ministry of Petroleum Industry (MPI) 11, 16-18, 20, 21, 89-91, 104, 125, 133
modernization 3, 8, 22, 53, 67, 68, 82, 92, 100, 115, 131, 139, 154, 157, 158

Official Development Assistance (ODA) 157

oil 1-6, 8-13, 15-32, 35-47, 50-55, 57-60, 62, 63, 65-80, 83-85, 87-91, 97, 100-102, 104-109, 111-118, 121-149, 151, 153-160
oilfield 1, 2, 4, 6, 8, 10-12, 14, 16, 20, 23, 25, 26, 31, 35, 37-40, 44-48, 50-52, 54, 58, 69, 72, 76, 77, 86-89, 91-93, 97-100, 105, 111, 113, 121, 126, 131, 134, 135, 137, 139, 145, 152, 154, 158
oil-deficient 123
Organization of Petroleum Exporting Countries (OPEC) 122, 140, 157

petroleum 6, 8, 11-22, 24, 27, 30, 31, 34, 36, 38, 39, 42, 45, 53, 54, 67-69, 72, 74-77, 79, 83, 84, 86-91, 96, 100-102, 104, 107, 108, 110, 111, 114, 116, 122, 124, 125, 127, 133, 134, 139, 140, 142, 144-148, 152-156, 158, 160
Petroleum Faction 8, 11, 12, 34, 79, 83, 84, 87, 88, 90, 91, 96, 100-102, 107, 108, 110, 114, 116, 139, 144-147, 152-154
pipeline 26, 45, 49, 74, 128-131, 134, 137, 139, 146
pipes 26, 32, 42, 44, 74, 129-131, 146

quota 36, 141, 142, 144

refinery 30, 41, 74, 128
reforms 115, 159
reliance 6, 61, 66, 74, 77, 80, 119, 121, 159
revisionism 85, 103
rig 75, 147

scientific 37, 39, 48, 62, 83, 97-99, 102, 105, 110, 115, 132
self-reliance 1-8, 11, 12, 25, 32, 36, 37, 41, 43, 44, 57-70, 72-75, 77, 95, 107, 109-111, 114, 115, 119, 153, 155, 157, 158
self-strengthening 3, 92
Sino-Japanese 1, 51, 59, 116-118, 123, 124, 127, 129, 130, 132, 135-138, 140, 141, 143, 144, 146, 149, 153-155
Sino-Soviet 8, 53, 59, 60, 65, 68, 70, 136, 158
Songliao 12-16, 23, 46, 50-52
steel 74, 107, 116, 117, 129-131, 142, 146
strategic 5, 61, 64, 105, 136, 139, 159

Taching 5, 6, 25, 26, 31, 47, 54, 58, 66, 88, 100-104
technocratic 3, 33, 36, 67, 80-83, 91, 92, 96, 100, 110, 114, 115
technologies 8, 61, 64, 68, 73, 74, 77, 109, 110, 113-115, 118, 119, 125, 135, 139, 142, 144, 155, 158